Acknowledgements

It is impossible to give full credit to everyone who has in some way contributed to this book because many of the ideas and activities described in the book are adaptations of things I've learned from others in workshops and courses over the past 25 years. Parts of this book appeared in **Field Trips: An Adventure in Learning,** a training guide I wrote a few years ago. I wish to again acknowledge and thank all the people who contributed to that publication, especially Laurel Goulding, Beth Overstad, Connie Koroglu, Zona Ivory, Erna Fishhaut and Sue Anne Williams. Most of the traditional fingerplays and verses included in that earlier publication and repeated in this one came from resources made available by the Minnesota Department of Public Welfare and the Minneapolis and St. Paul Public Schools' curriculum departments long, long ago.

In addition, there are several people who deserve special recognition for their important roles in bringing this book to fruition. I am exceedingly grateful for all their help and wish to express sincere thanks to:

—Deb Fish, Director of Development, whose faith, interest, prodding and production know-how made this book a reality!

—Susan Middleton, Editor, whose amazing talent for polishing up all the rough edges as well as any overlong or confused sentences is evidenced throughout this book, with the exception of these acknowledgements, as you can tell!

—Connie Koroglu, Illustrator, whose outstanding illustrations and design are readily apparent, but whose creativity, meticulousness and diligence have contributed so very much more.

—The staff of the St. Paul Public Library Children's Room, and St. Anthony Park Branch Library, who helped me ferret out books for some of these unusual topics as well as assisting Connie in finding resources for her illustrations.

—Zona Ivory, who patiently waded through endless changes in copy and illegible notes up the sides of pages, always with a cheerful smile, and still managed to find the inconsistencies resulting from my poor memory.

—Beth Overstad and Jane Heille who helped proofread final copy, along with offering other help along the way.

—My family, who put up with and even encouraged my writing on vacations, weekends and the wee hours since I was always behind schedule, and listened enthusiastically to my songs and fingerplays even when they weren't interested. Eric, and especially Karen, were better at remembering verses I made up in the car or other unlikely places than I was, and several of these may well have been lost forever without their help.

and especially . . .

—My husband, Paul, whose constant support and encouragement has made this all possible.

Contents

MORE FIELD TRIP IDEAS

ESPECIALLY FOR TEACHERS

SUGGESTED RESOURCES

Introduction

This book is designed to open the door to learning, not only for children, but for parents and teachers as well. Often in our eagerness to expose young children to the wonders of our technological society, we overlook the learning potential of common, ordinary, everyday experiences. The most important learning task facing young children remains that of "making sense of their world," and the adults in their lives are the tour guides to that world. Adults provide the bridges from the known to the unknown for the children they teach. It is hoped that this book will provide both assistance and stimulation in furthering that process.

The trips described here are expansions on activities which are readily available in the daily lives of children everywhere, but which often are not recognized as "learning activities." These experiences become exciting new learning adventures to the extent that adults (parents and teachers) make them so. Just as our own experiences exploring a new country or a new location are enhanced by a guide who points things out to us, and gives us just the right amount of information to stimulate our interest and curiosity, so are the children's explorations of the new (and even not so new) sites in their world enhanced by adult guidance. The trick is "just the right amount" of information, questioning and stimulation. The following suggestions for using this book should aid you in making those judgements.

This book contains a wealth of ideas and activities associated with various field trips, from which adults can choose those that best fit their children's needs and interests. It is intended as a resource for adults and not as a recipe book to be followed to the letter. Each trip lists several purposes one might consider for that trip. Trips could easily be repeated on different occasions to meet different purposes, depending on the children's ages and interest levels. The activities one chooses to pursue before, during and after a particular trip should relate to the specific purpose or purposes of that trip.

Each trip includes a large list of words, randomly selected, that could be associated with that trip. Again, the adults should choose from that list the half dozen or so new words they hope to emphasize and help the children understand. These will vary considerably depending on the ages and vocabularies the children bring to the trip, and again can be added to on repeat trips. The three-year-old will be learning very basic names and descriptive words. The five-year-old will be learning more technical terms and words related to concepts.

Each trip follows the same basic pattern. This is important in that it exemplifies the thought process one should use in planning trips for children: consider your purpose, think of the words you will be emphasizing, plan the ways in which you get ready for and introduce the trip idea, think about the things to do along the way that further your purposes and enhance learning, and plan a variety of follow-up activities as the continuation and reinforcement of that learning. To round out the experience, include fingerplays, songs and books to read and look at. The trip thus becomes a focal point in an integrated learning process, rather than an added-on activity of unclear relevance to the children.

Included with each trip are original fingerplays and songs, a few old favorites, as well as some listings of additional fingerplays and songs from a very limited number of outside sources. Selected books of fingerplays and songs, and general resource books listed in the annotated bibliography at the end of the book offer many additional good choices. Some of these trips had large numbers of fingerplays and songs available, and including all appropriate ones was impossible. Other topics had no songs or fingerplays available. It was for this reason that I chose to write original songs and fingerplays for all trips, and to omit many favorite and very useable ones. The book lists accompanying each trip presented some of the same challenges as the fingerplays and songs. It was either feast or famine. However, the solution of creating books to accompany these trips was not a viable option. Hence some of the books included on some topics are not really preschool-level books and should be used for their pictures and general information and adapted as appropriate.

I have not included a special listing of records and audio-visual materials for each trip because these materials are not as generally available as books. However, a number of favorite children's stories, particularly on nature topics, are available as film strips with cassette tapes. If your library or school has these available, by all means use them in addition to books. There are a number of excellent records available under the Young People's Records, Children's Record Guild and Bowmar labels which would be useful with several of these field trips, particularly the nature ones. Again, I encourage you to check on their availability in your community.

The opening section of this book includes some general information about how children learn, which is intended to set the stage for the trips that follow. The final section includes a number of suggestions concerning the mechanics of planning field trips which will generally be useful to teachers and child care providers. The reader is encouraged to make use of these forms, lists and suggestions in any way they wish. They may be copied by teachers to use with parents or in their own planning.

EXPERIENCE AND LEARNING

Field Trips: An Approach to Learning

Trips give adults an opportunity to see for themselves something they have heard or read about. Trips serve not only that same function for children, but also its opposite. They give children an opportunity to see for themselves something they will learn more about later in pictures or books or through conversation. Children learn to make sense of the world around them through many different experiences. The greater the quantity and variety of experiences, the greater the learning potential.

While books, pictures, filmstrips and television provide information for children, it is only two-dimensional and secondhand, and is no substitute for the real thing! Young children have limited experiences and understanding of the world. Because of this, they do not have the background or skill to use secondhand sources of information effectively. Think of the difference between seeing a picture of an ice cream sundae and eating a real ice cream sundae. If we've only seen pictures or heard about ice cream, our notion of what ice cream is will be very different than if we've eaten the real thing. It is easy to see that people who have *eaten* ice cream have a different level of understanding of that concept, than people who've only *read* or *heard* about ice cream. The same principle is true for all concepts that children are learning. Children need to use all their senses to gain an undistorted view of the world. The more exposure children have to firsthand experiences, the richer their understanding becomes. A look at the world through the eyes of a child can help parents and teachers find valuable material for learning right under their noses.

The first field trip may well be taken around a familiar room. This trip offers any child from infant to preschooler a chance to notice and learn the names of all the things in the room. Be sure to look at not just toys, but also furniture, pipes, heat registers, wall and floor composition. For a baby, simple words such as chair, table and window can be mentioned. For older children, more details should be named, such as *rocking* chair, or *leather* chair, *round* table or *dining room* table, and window sill. The next trip might be a further exploration of the house or building, such as a visit to the kitchen to explore the appliances and pipes, and down to the basement to see where those pipes go. In a school or center, children could visit the office area to look at the machines, special furniture or equipment.

After looking closely at rooms within the house or building, it is time to explore the neighborhood. Every neighborhood contains many opportunities to explore and learn if we are alert to the little things we adults take for granted. There are many common and obvious things that children may never have had explained to them: the way sidewalks are made, puddles and where the water goes, trees and how they change, and so on. Every group should pick a favorite tree that they visit once a week in the fall to see how it changes, with visits at intervals during winter and spring. The children can contrast "their" tree with another tree down the block. Encourage children to touch the tree and feel the different textures, and to smell the sap in the living branches. Houses, cars, people, animals, nature, and much more can all be observed and studied on walks around the block.

From the immediate neighborhood we can move on to the larger community, its services and resources. Lucky is the home or program that is within walking distance of a service station, grocery store or other general shopping area. The world becomes a more accessible "oyster" for them. Others may need to use transportation (public, car pool or school bus) to explore their community. Each family or group must weigh for themselves which parts of the community are most readily available to them. Many parents and teachers overlook the possibility of public transportation, but going on a bus in itself is an exciting experience for many children. Naturally, safety, convenience and monetary factors must all be weighed in making choices.

The same site can be visited many times, but for a different purpose each time. Each visit becomes a unique experience because of that different purpose. A trip to the grocery store can be taken on one occasion to see how food is organized and arranged, another time to observe what people do and how the store "works." A third trip may be used to put these observations to use by having the children shop for a cooking project. Revisiting a site will allow the children to gain more mature insights because of what has been learned in the interim.

Excursions offer many opportunities to name objects and activities, which will in turn have an immediate impact by enlarging children's vocabularies. But, in our eagerness to give information, it is easy to overlook the value of asking questions, such as, "I wonder what that squirrel is doing?" or "What do you suppose is in that package the mail carrier is delivering?" This questioning approach plays an important role in learning. It develops the children's curiosity and problem-solving skills. By offering children clues to use in their guesses, such as the size of the package, the adult is demonstrating a logical thinking technique. This approach is worth using even though it may produce "silly" answers from children at some developmental stages.

To maximize the value of an excursion, it is necessary to plan preparatory and follow-up experiences, so that the new knowledge can become integrated with what the child already knows. Children should be informed of details to look for while on the trip. They can rehearse the trip, thus making them more self-assured. After the trip the children will need opportunities to use the new concepts they've learned and to state in their own words what they've experienced. Listen to what the children say and how they react to the experience. Don't be surprised if they are impressed with something the adults have never even noticed. That's what makes field trips such a rewarding experience for both children and adults.

A "field trip" is not just a trip to the zoo in a bus or car, although that is certainly one type of field trip, too often the only type we think of. A field trip is more a frame of mind, an approach to an experience either indoors or out, that focuses attention on inquiry:

—on noticing things in more or less detail depending on the child's age;

—on comparing or contrasting new things to other known or familiar objects or experiences;

—on wondering how things get to be where and what they are and what they do;

—on describing and talking about things seen;

—and on enjoying and learning from our environment.

From this point of view it becomes clear that field trips have a valuable role to play in helping children learn. They help children:

—develop an awareness of surroundings and sharpen observation skills;

—correct misunderstandings and gain new information;

4

—build vocabularies through concrete experience;

—join in group discussions stimulated by the field trip experience;

—create new ideas for use in dramatic play;

—increase their understanding of seasonal changes, and the role of nature;

—find collections of things to study or use for art projects;

—observe the way people live and work and how the community functions;

—get exercise needed for growing bodies and minds;

—become aware of the scientific method of inquiry;

and besides all that, the field trips MIGHT JUST HAPPEN TO BE FUN!

What Is Learning Anyway and What Does It Have to Do With Going on a Walk?

Children naturally seek out experiences that will expand their understanding of the world and themselves. They are learning all the time, from everything around them. Their thoughts develop from their interactions with people, objects and events. It is through numerous and varied direct experiences that children learn to make sense of the world. This active physical and mental involvement works to enhance children's ability to pay attention, to remember, and ultimately to understand their world as well as the things they encounter in it. The early learning process can be divided into four components which continually interact and reinforce each other.

1. **Perception:** The learning process begins with direct sensory experiences. To learn about something, children must be able to perceive it—to take it in through their senses. For example, the child who is blind is unable to understand the qualities of color. From infancy on, children look at, listen to, touch, smell and taste the things in their environment, in order to learn about them. As they get older, children push, pull, twist, manipulate and actively explore things for the same reason. There are a multitude of things in the environment and no one can pay attention to everything at once. To learn, the child must selectively pay attention to some things, and ignore others. The events most likely to capture a child's attention are those with which the child is somewhat familiar. If a new experience is unrelated to what the child already understands, the child may ignore it. Young children and adults frequently pay attention to different features of a situation. Adults can help children sort out the important and unimportant features of a learning situation. They can supply the names of patterns or events to be perceived. Rather than giving children lots of information, adults can teach them to be observant by asking pertinent questions and helping to focus their attention.

2. **Language:** Language is not essential to learning or thinking, but it can aid the process. The development of language helps a young child think, and developing new ways of thinking helps the child learn language. When learning the name of an object, the child is forced to attend to the features that distinguish that object from others. Young children first learn to understand words that name specific objects or actions. Words that represent concepts or conditions (big, round, soft), rather than objects, present more difficulty to the child and only become understood through repeated exposure to those concepts in a variety of contexts. Hardest of all are the words that are used to relate objects to each other such as underneath, behind, over, and so on. Children who have learned the names for relationships are better prepared to solve problems than other children. Adults can aid this process by providing children with many opportunities to talk and to listen. They can supply new vocabulary and encourage children to generalize, and state things in their own words. Adults can provide good examples of language every time they speak to children.

3. **Memory:** Memory affects learning. Learning of new information is related to what the child already knows. New information is compared with things that are familiar to the child, evaluated and stored in memory for further use. The more children understand, the more new information they can learn and remember. Generally speaking, older children have better memory skills than younger children and can therefore learn and retain more readily. Because young children have a limited ability to absorb and recall new information, repetition can be in the form of repeated exposure to the same new material in several different forms or ways. Young children generally remember if they are actively involved in what is to be learned. Children can be encouraged to recall new experiences by pretending to be something they have seen, felt, heard, touched or smelled. Children also remember new information better if it is organized in some manner. In short, the development of memory skill can best be facilitated by encouraging children to actively explore the world around them, presenting new information in small doses, repeating it in a variety of contexts, and providing "bridges" that link new and old information.

4. **Logical Thinking:** Children can, and do, learn without any formal teaching. The rate of the development of logical thinking varies, depending on the child and the experiences the environment offers. But all children progress through stages of thinking in the same sequence. This popular theory, developed by Jean Piaget, suggests that young children are unable to comprehend logical principles. Piaget believes that older children do not simply know more than younger children. They think in different ways. Children learn best when they are ready to learn, and understanding develops from the active manipulation of materials and the observation of resulting changes. Piaget does not believe it is possible to speed up the development of logical thinking, but his theory suggests that offering a variety of opportunities to practice new concepts will enhance the child's breadth and depth of understanding at each stage. Adults can help children organize what they know into logical groupings. Specific skills develop slowly, as the children experience and practice them and use them in their world of play.

Direct experiences with real things in the outside world (sometimes called field trips) play an important role in this continually interactive process of children's learning. But the extent to which these experiences become effective teaching tools will be dependent on the way parents or teachers structure and interpret them. As the children walk along it is important to:

—emphasize the sensory experiences around them by touching the grass and bark, smelling the flowers, listening to the cars and the wind;

—name the things they are seeing and talk about them in detail, such as the colors and shapes of different leaves, the parts of the houses, the signs along the road;

—help the children recall the things they've seen before and how these relate to things they are seeing now, like shrubs that resemble an evergreen tree they've seen, or a collie who has longer hair and is bigger than the poodle they know;

—encourage thinking about how and why things happen by wondering what the squirrels are doing running up and down the oak tree and why there are so many leaves piling up on the ground in fall.

The learning process is greatly influenced by the child's attitudes and feelings. Children who have had some successes and feel self-confident will be more able to cope with new learning situations. Feelings about learning are also influenced by relationships with others. Children who feel they are liked and valued as people will want to become involved in learning. Adults can support children's learning by paying attention to their efforts, treating their questions with respect and giving encouragement and approval. They can help children learn to cope with disappointment, frustration and failure, since true learning will always include periods of failure on the road to mastery.

Some Questions to Ask Yourself in Planning Trips

Making the Experience More Meaningful

Any experience that a young child has will make a deeper impression and last longer if it is reinforced. There are a number of simple techniques for doing this. These techniques will also make the trip more enjoyable, and the children will be more easily guided on the trip. When preparing for a trip, ask yourself:

What things are the children already familiar with which relate to the new ideas, concepts and experiences they will be exposed to?

What ways are there to act out or dramatize the experience before and after the trip?

What opportunities will I have, or can I make, to talk about the experience before, during, and after the trip?

How can I encourage the children to talk about the experience before, during, and after?

In what ways can I expect the children to show their interest, reactions, or excitement on this particular trip? What can I do to reinforce these feelings?

What secondary images (photographs, television, movies, books, displays) are available to reinforce the experience?

What new social experiences will the children have and how can I plan to make them healthy experiences?

What kinds of sensory experiences are available on this field trip?

What related experiences can I plan before and after the trip?

Although most of us can immediately think of one or two potential learning experiences for every trip, there are always many more hidden possibilities; and some child is bound to bump into one. Prior thought will help prepare us to respond immediately to the child's discovery in a manner which builds on spontaneous interest.

THE WONDERFUL WORLD OF WALKS

After-a-Rain Walk

notice the effect of rain on trees in spring, fall.....

learn about puddles.

observe where water goes.

look for rain bows.....

float twigs in little rivulets of water.....

notice the changes that water causes

observe worms.....

Some Words to Learn and Use

rain   thunder   lightning   clouds   fog   damp   drizzle

shower   rainbow   puddle   moisture   evaporate

absorb   earthworm   mud   sewer   drain   storm

umbrella/raincoat   water repellent   soak

Read a Story

Read **Where Does the Butterfly Go When it Rains?**. Ask the children where they think the butterfly goes when it rains. Ask the children what they've noticed about rain; what happens to trees, grass, pavement. Make a list of questions about rain to investigate on your walk.

Do and Experiment

Experiment with water using an eyedropper and a variety of materials such as stones, feathers, grass and leaves. Drop water on the objects and observe what happens. Discuss what happens to the water and the materials. Plan to go outside to see more things after a rain.

On the Walk / Ideas for Exploring

Observing

Look at and touch trees and bushes to see how they appear and feel. Shake some branches to see what happens.

Look for spots where puddles have collected and see if you can figure out why. Ask the children how long the puddles might be there.

Sensing

Notice the air around you—take some deep breaths and sniffs. How does it feel? Is it cool, hot, muggy, humid, fresh, windy, or sunny? You might remember to look out while it's raining to see what the weather looked like during the storm; then try to recall and contrast the conditions outside after the rain.

Look at and/or touch cars, grass, dirt, sidewalks, things left outside (playground equipment, toys, sandbox) to see what evidence is left of the rain. Dig in the dirt to see how wet it is on top and further down. Notice if there are places where there is no evidence of any rain having fallen and wonder why.

Experimenting

Look for places where the water is moving and try to figure out what makes it move. Put some little twigs in the moving water to see what happens. Put a large rock in its path to see what happens. Can you stop the water? Watch the water run down the sewer if possible.

Look for worms and observe them. Dig in the dirt to see if there are any worms. Are there more worms on the sidewalk or in the dirt? What happens to the worms left on the sidewalk?

Talking About

Ask the children about the things they notice or want to ask about while on the walk.

Set a limit on and discuss where you are walking down to the corner, around the block, or to the playground and back.

Talk about setting up a special table area for experiments with water after you return. Plan to try different ones over the next few days.

After the Walk / Follow-up Activities

Discussion

Talk about the walk. Let the children share their experiences.

Discuss rain and storms and make a book about weather.

Ask the children why it rains. What would happen if there were no rain?

Rainy Day Mural

Make a large rainy day mural using a variety of materials (cotton for clouds, fabric for raincoats and umbrellas, clear plastic for puddles, silver rick-rack for lightning, styrofoam squiggles painted brown for worms).

Evaporation

Put water in a pie tin. Let it sit out for a few days. Observe what happens. Discuss evaporation.

Return to see a puddle later or the next day. Ask what happened to the puddle.

Make Rain

How about making rain? Heat water in tea kettle until it boils. Hold a cold plate over the spout so steam hits the plate. When lots of drops have formed on plate, let children feel it and talk about how it feels. If the plate got really full of drops, what would the drops do?

Absorption

Do experiments with water and different materials (sugar, sand, dirt) to see what happens.

Fill baby food jars half full with dry materials. Add a layer of water and shake. Observe what happens. Let jars stand a while and observe again. Try many different dry materials and types of dirt and discuss which ones hold water the longest. Which ones would be best for plants?

Umbrella Salad

Have an umbrella salad for lunch or snack. Cut a slice of canned pineapple in half. Make stem by cutting bananas in half and slicing the long way. Put maraschino cherries on top of pineapple (in center) to decorate umbrella.

14

Rain Coats

Drop water from an *eye dropper* onto different fabrics. Discover which fabrics offer good protection from water and would make a good raincoat.

Egg Carton Umbrellas

Make umbrellas out of *egg cartons* and *pipe cleaners* (like upside down tulips). Hang on tree branch or on bulletin board.

Worms

Dig in the ground for worms on a hot, dry summer day and again after a heavy rain. Wonder together about why the worms are easier to find after rain. Talk about who uses worms and when would be a good time to look for them.

Float and Sink

Take some things outside to float in the puddles and little streams formed after a rain. Notice which things float and which don't. (Take along twigs, bits of wood, styrofoam, nails, bottle caps, pennies.) Collect the things that float in one container and the things that don't in another. Write a little story about the experiment after you get inside. Guess what makes things float.

Pro and Con Chart

Make up a pro and con chart about rain. Have children finish the sentences: "I like rain because" and "I don't like rain because."

Buoyancy Demonstration

Discuss the concept of buoyancy using this demonstration to help in the explanation. Use a large container of water filled to the brim. Set inside a pan. Take a rock with a rope around and immerse it so the water overflows into the pan. Weigh the rock on one side of a balance scale and the water that overflowed on the other side. Use wood, rock, styrofoam. When the object weighs more than the same amount of water, it sinks. When it weighs less than the same amount of water, it floats. When the object weighs the same as the amount of water it displaces, it floats half-way down, producing "neutral buoyancy." *Gravity* is a *pulling down* force. *Buoyancy* is a *pushing up* force.

Songs, Poems and Fingerplays

Rain and Thunder

To the tune of "Frere Jacque"

Rain and thunder, rain and thunder,
Boom, boom, boom; boom, boom, boom.   *Clap hands*
See the flash of lightning,
Oh, my, it is frightening,
Boom, boom, boom; boom, boom, boom.   *Clap hands*

To the tune of "Twinkle, Twinkle, Little Star"

Rain is Falling

Pitter, patter, little drops,
Rain is falling, never stops.
On the windows and the roofs,
Like the sound of little hoofs,
Pitter, patter, splash the drops,
The raining noises never stop.

A Rain Story

Traditional

Pitter, patter, pitter, patter,   *Use fingers on table or floor to make sound*
Hear the raindrops say,
But if a sunbeam should peep out,   *Touch fingers overhead to make rainbow*
They'd make a rainbow gay.

Rumble, rumble, rumble, rumble,   *Move fist and let knuckles make rumble sound on table or floor*
Hear the thunder say,
Soon the clouds will be all gone,   *Move hands behind back*
And we'll go out to play.

Traditional

Thunder

Black clouds are giants,
Hurrying across the sky,
And they slip out bolts of lightning,
As they go racing by.

When they meet each other,
They shake hands and thunder,
How-do-you-do, how-do-you-do,
HOW-DO-YOU-DOOOOOOO.

16

And more

Tis Raining, It's Raining on the Town,, Puddles, from **Songs for the Nursery School.** Laura Pendleton MacCarteney, Willis, 1937.

Japanese Rain Song, from **Sing a Song.** Lucille Wood and Roberta MacLaughlin, Prentice-Hall, 1960.

Raindrops, The Rain, from **Rhymes for Fingers and Flannelboards.** Louise Scott and J. J. Thompson, McGraw-Hill, 1960.

Books

Bartlett, Margaret F. **Where Does All the Rain Go?** Coward, 1974.

Branley, Franklyn. **Rain and Hail.** Crowell, 1963.

Brandt, Keith. **What Makes It Rain: the Story of a Raindrop.** Troll, 1982.

Broekel, Ray. **Storms (The New True Book of).** Childrens Press, 1982.

Carrick, Donald. **Drip, Drop.** MacMillan, 1973.

Darling, Lois and Louis. **Worms.** Morrow, 1972.

Edwards, Dorothy. **A Wet Monday.** Morrow, 1976.

Foster, Joanna. **Pete's Puddle.** Harcourt Brace, 1950.

Garelick, May. **Where Does the Butterfly Go When it Rains.** Addison-Wesley, 1961.

Ginsburg, Mirra. **Mushroom in the Rain.** MacMillan, 1974.

Goudey, Alice. **Good Rain.** Dutton, 1950.

Lukesova, Milena. **The Little Girl and the Rain.** Harper & Row, 1978.

Morgan, Shirley. **Rain, Rain Don't Go Away.** Dutton, 1972.

Parsons, Ellen. **Rainy Day Together.** Harper & Row, 1971.

Ryder, Joanne. **A Wet and Sandy Day.** Harper & Row, 1977.

Scheer, Julian. **Rain Makes Applesauce.** Holiday House, 1964.

Schlein, Miriam. **The Sun, The Wind, The Sea and The Rain.** Abelard-Schuman, 1960.

Shulevitz, Uri. **Rain, Rain Rivers.** Farrar Straus, 1969.

Tresselt, Alvin. **Rain-Drop Splash.** Lothrop, 1946.

...look for living creatures...

Animal Life Walk

learn about insects and small animals...

...observe their characteristics...

...see their homes...collect different types of insects...

Some Words to Learn and Use

animal   living   plant   mammal   pet   dog   puppy
cat   kitten   rabbit   squirrel   mouse   fur   hair
warm-blooded   species   invertebrate   bird   reptile
amphibian   insect   worm   spider   lady bug   bee
beetle   butterfly   moth   ant   mosquito   fly
grasshopper   colony   nest   skeleton   feelers
antennae   eyes   legs   wings   tail   mouth   ears
paws   sting   egg-laying   live-bearing   life cycle
cocoon   change   caterpillar   metamorphosis   web

Before the Walk / Introductory Activities

Talk About

Ask the children if they have any pets. Let them tell you about their pets. Find out what kind of pets they have and discuss where the pets stay. Do they have any special types of living arrangements for their pets? What do their pets eat? Do their pets go outside and what do they do when they are outside? Talk about what other living creatures might be found outside besides pets. Wonder what they eat and if they have special living arrangements. Make a list of all the different types of insects and small animals you might see on a walk.

Make Bug Boxes

Make bug boxes to take on your walk so the children can collect some insects if they wish. (See "After the Walk" section for directions.)

Look at Pictures

Look at pictures of insects, birds and mammals. Notice some of the identifying characteristics. The **Golden Science** books, the **New True** books, the **Time-Life** books and the **Amazing World** books (see book list) all have beautiful pictures. Encyclopedias are also good sources of pictures. Talk about the particular types of insects, birds or small animals you might find in your neighborhood at this time of year. Plan to look again at other times of year as well.

On the Walk / Ideas for Exploring

Observing

Look for pets that might be outside. Do you see any pets besides cats and dogs? Are the animals running free, on a leash, in a fenced-in area, or tied up? Think about why that might be. What are they doing? Notice the sizes of the animals and decide if any of them are still puppies or kittens. Notice the different ways the animals move and behave.

Look for other forms of animal life besides pets, such as squirrels, rabbits, birds, insects. Notice their body parts, how they move and how they eat. Do you see them looking for food? Bring along some bread crumbs to help facilitate your observations.

Look for signs of animal life even when you can't see the animals. Do you see any dog houses, holes in trees, birds' nests, ant hills, mole holes and so on? Look for footprints and tracks in the mud or snow.

Sensing

Listen for the sounds the animals make. Have the children close their eyes and listen. Can they tell what animals might be around just by the sounds they hear?

Listen for sounds other than vocalizations associated with animal life, such as rustling of bushes or trees, pecking on wood, or flapping of wings.

If there are pets or insects that can be touched, feel the different textures of the body coverings. Talk about what makes them feel the way they do.

Identifying

Name as many different kinds of creatures as you can. Try to identify them as members of a specific category, such as birds, but also as a specific kind of bird, such as robin. Bring along a few small picture guides of birds, insects, or dogs which might help you in the identification process.

Call attention to body parts and features which can help you make identifications. For birds: call attention to coloring, markings, shape of head, body, wings and bill, eye rings and stripes. For dogs: notice general size, length of legs and hair, shape of head, ears, body, facial features, tail, coloring and markings. For insects: look for the number of legs, location of antennae, size and shape of body and wings, coloring and so on. It might be helpful to bring along a magnifying glass to use in looking at insects.

Compare various forms of animal life as to number of legs, type of covering such as fur, hair, skin or feathers, sizes, ways in which it moves and behaves. Don't forget the large-sized animals we call "people."

Speculating

Wonder where the different creatures live at different times of year. What do they do in the winter time? Do they need shelter all the time, or just while they have babies? Wonder if they live in families or groups of their own. How do they feed their babies?

Think about what foods the creatures eat and wonder how they find their food. Do they have trouble finding food at some times of the year and what do they do about it? Can we help?

How do the creatures protect themselves from each other? Do they fight or bother each other?

Plan to observe animal life at different seasons of the year to gather more information on these questions. Collect some insects in your bug boxes to take back and observe as well.

After the Walk / Follow-up Activities

Discussion

Talk about the things you observed on your walk and make some generalizations about the creatures in your neighborhood. Examples: All the dogs are on leashes, all birds around here are called pigeons, or there are lots of different kinds of birds.

Talk about what functions some of the creatures serve. Decide if there are some which are really harmful or are they just pests? Think about degrees of harm and good as with bees who, though they may sting us, also help the flowers bloom, or give honey. Think about mosquitoes and flies who spread diseases, bite and annoy us, whose only redeeming feature may be providing food for birds, frogs, and other larger creatures.

Look at books and review some basic categories of animal life so the children get some very simple notion of classification and differentiation among classes of animal life.

Make Lotto Games

Using a variety of animal seals or pictures from wrapping paper, make animal lotto games. Use them to play games for small groups or as a sorting activity for individual children.

Make Matching Games

Cut out pictures of animals and animal homes. Let the children match the animal to its home.

Mount pictures of animals, birds, insects on tag board. Draw or cut out other pictures of animal body parts such as antennae, tails, wings, facial features and so on. Mount these on small cards. Children match the body part to the appropriate animal, bird or insect.

Story Book About Pets

Make up a large story book about children's pets. Include information about pets from babyhood to old age. For instance, include pictures and comments about puppies in a litter, how puppies behave, how mature and old dogs behave. At each stage of development include anecdotes about the children's own pets who are at that stage. Dog food or other animal products will have pictures of animals at different stages. Or use real life pictures. Have different sections in the book deal with different types of pets.

Make Number Ladybugs

Make ladybugs to use in talking about circles and numbers. Cut two large circles for each ladybug. Cut one of the large circles in half to serve as the wings of the ladybug, and attach both sections to the whole circle using a brass fastener. The fastener should be large enough to allow the halves to open or close. Make the large circles out of red or orange paper. Cut lots of small circles out of black paper. Paste one black circle to each ladybug for its head. Use the other circles to paste onto the wings, varying the number of circles on each ladybug so that you can use them for number games.

Make some ladybugs with the same amount of dots on each wing (from one - five) and some with different amounts on each wing. Play games such as find the ladybugs with *five* dots, or find the ladybug with *three* dots on each wing. Have one child place cut-out numerals on the body under the wings indicating how many dots are on the wings. Another child looks under to see if the number is correct.

Creative Dramatics

Make a variety of animal headbands such as rabbit ears. Have the children wear the headbands and imitate the actions of the animals: rabbits hopping, dogs running, or frogs jumping. Many of the songs found in the resource list are ideal for dramatization.

Set up an animal fair using a variety of paper bag costumes for the children to wear and design different settings for the "pretend" animals.

Chairs or boxes can be used as cages or habitats. Some children can pretend to be the animals, while others come to watch the animals or to feed them.

Book Display

Set up a table display. Set out lots of books with animal pictures in them. Read animal stories. Let the children dramatize some of the stories such as the "Angus" or "Mousekin" stories.

Something for the Birds

Bird Feeders

Have children mix together one part margarine to one part peanut butter. Twist wire around a pine cone to form a loop for hanging. Spread peanut butter mixture over the pine cone with a knife. Roll in bird seed or cereal crumbs. Hang outside.

Poke holes in a paper cup in several spots. Also poke a pair of holes at the top of the cup to use for string or wire for hanging. Poke still another pair at the bottom in which to insert a small stick for birds to use as a perch. Other holes should be above the perch area. Fill the cup with a mixture of peanut butter, bread crumbs, bird seed and apple bits. Tie string or wire to top and hang from tree branches.

Or set out a commercially made bird feeder and keep it stocked with food.

Make Egg Carton Creatures

Make a variety of insects or small animals using egg carton sections. Decorate the creatures with cut paper ears, wings, feet and pipe cleaner whiskers or feelers.

Animal Category Game

Cut several sheets of 8" by 10" tagboard. On each one, draw a large picture of a setting where creatures might be found: a yard, woods, house, farm or zoo. Cut out a number of pictures of the creatures that might be found in those settings. Children sort the pictures according to where the animals or insects might be found.

Caterpillar Life Cycle Chart

Make a chart of the life cycle of a caterpillar from caterpillar to butterfly. Talk about the life cycle of other insects.

Make Bug Boxes

To make a bug box, cut the top portion of a plastic dish detergent bottle and make a few openings along the sides of the lower section. Insert the remaining plastic bottle into a section of nylon stocking, making sure there are no holes in the part of the stocking that covers the openings in the bottle. Leave about 6-8" of stocking hanging loose above the bottle for the children to hold. It is not necessary to knot the stocking. To use, the children simply spread the stocking open, roll it down a bit and drop the bug inside.

Have Animals Visit

Get a hamster, guinea pig, rabbit or other small animal from the "visiting animal program" of a zoo; or purchase a small animal you would like to care for from a pet store. Guinea pigs are easier for children to handle and care for than some other animals. They are also easier to find if they get out of their cages.

Songs, Poems and Fingerplays

Oh Did You Hear?

To the tune of "The Muffin Man"

Oh did you hear the doggies bark?
The doggies bark, the doggies bark.
Oh did you hear the doggies bark
When you went out today?

Oh yes we heard the doggies bark
The doggies bark, the doggies bark.
Oh yes we heard the doggies bark
And this is what they say:

Children imitate dog sounds

(Additional animals to use:)
Oh did you hear the kittens mew?
Oh did you hear the birdies sing?
Oh did you hear the froggies croak?

Children make the appropriate sound after each sequence

One Little Ant

One little ant crept out to play
Out from his little hill one day.
He had such enormous fun
He called for another little ant to come.

Two little ants crept out to play
Out from their little hill one day.
They had such enormous fun
They called for another little ant to come.

Adapted from "One Elephant Went Out to Play"

Children can hold up fingers for each number; or use as a circle game and have one child pick another for each new number

Traditional

Hands together with palms curved
Wrap one hand around the other fist
Form large circle by joining tips of thumb and first finger
Join fingertips to form roof

Here is a Nest

Here is a nest for a robin,
Here is a hive for a bee,
Here is a hole for a rabbit,
And here is a home for me.

Pretty Little Kitty

Pretty little Kitty sniffed
At a rose.
Along came a bumble bee
And stung her nose.
Poor little Kitty said "Meow,"
"Look how funny my nose looks now!"

Hold up thumb on one hand and sniff with nose

Other hand stings nose

Point to nose

I'd Like to Be

I'd like to be a bunny
And hop and hop all day.
I'd like to be a little pup
And run and run and play.
I'd like to be a birdie
And fly and fly so high.
I'd like to be a buzzy bee
And buzz and swoop and fly.
I'd like to be so many things
That I see out my door.
But really I'm a little child
That sits down on the floor.

Children hop

Children run

Imitate flying

Make a buzzing sound and swoop hands

Look outside

Children sit down

And more

Ten Little Frogs, A Green Frog, Easter Bunny, from **Singing Fun.** Lucille Wood and Louise Scott. Webster, 1954.

Chase Your Tail, Kitty, Worm, Pussy Jumps High, Pussy Jumps Low, Pretty Little Bunny, Hop, Little Bunny, Fly Away Little Birdie, Zumm! Zumm! Zumm! and more from **Songs for the Nursery School.** Laura Pendelton MacCarteney. Willis, 1937.

Books

Allen, Gertrude. **Everyday Insects.** Houghton-Mifflin, 1963.

Barlowe, Dot and Sy. **Who Lives Here?** Random House, 1978.

Branley, Franklyn. **Big Tracks, Little Tracks.** Scholastic, 1960.

Brickloe, Julie. **The Spider's Web.** Doubleday, 1974.

Cameron, Polly. **I Can't Said the Ant.** Coward, 1961.

Carle, Eric. **Do You Want to be My Friend?** Crowell, 1971.

Carle, Eric. **Have You Seen My Cat?** Watts, 1973.

Carle, Eric. **The Grouchy Ladybug.** Crowell, 1977.

Carle, Eric. **The Very Hungry Caterpillar.** Collins, 1969.

Cook, Gladys Emerson. **Big Book of Cats.** Grosset & Dunlap, 1954.

Day, Jennifer. **What Is a Bird? Golden Science Book.** Western, 1975.

Day, Jennifer. **What Is a Mammal? Golden Science Book.** Western, 1975.

Day, Jennifer. **What Is an Insect? Golden Science Book.** Western, 1976.

Dunn, Judy. **The Little Rabbit.** Random House, 1980.

Fisher, Aileen. **Listen Rabbit.** Crowell, 1964.

Fisher, Aileen. **We Went Looking.** Crowell, 1968.

Fisher, Aileen. **Where Does Everyone Go?** Crowell, 1961.

Flack, Marjorie. **Angus and the Cat.** Doubleday, 1971.

Flack, Marjorie. **Angus and the Ducks.** Doubleday, 1930.

Green, Margaret. **Big Book of Pets.** Watts, 1966.

Hawes, Judy. **Bees and Beelines.** Crowell, 1964.

Hawes, Judy. **Fireflies in the Night.** Crowell, 1963.

Hawes, Judy. **Watch Honey Bees With Me.** Crowell, 1964.

Isenhart, Hans Heinrich. **A Duckling is Born.** Putnam, 1981.

Lionni, Leo. **Frederick.** Pantheon, 1967.

Lionni, Leo. **Inch by Inch.** Honor, 1962.

Lubell, Winifred and Cecil. **The Tall Grass Zoo.** Rand McNally, 1960.

Miller, Edna. **Mousekin's A.B.C.** Prentice-Hall, 1972.

Miller, Edna. **Mousekin's Woodland Sleepers.** Prentice-Hall, 1970.

Mitchell, Robert S. and Herbert S. Zim. **Butterflies and Moths.** Western, 1964.

Mizumura, Kazue. **If I Were A Cricket.** Crowell, 1973.

Mizumura, Kazue. **Way of an Ant.** Crowell, 1970.

Nakatani, Chiyoko. **The Zoo in My Garden.** Crowell, 1973.

Pfoog, Jan. **Kittens Are Like That.** Random House, 1976.

Peicewicz, Ann Thomas. **See What I Caught.** Prentice-Hall, 1974.

Podendorf, Illa. **Spiders (New True Book of).** Childrens Press, 1982.

Pope, Donna Lugge. **A Gerbil for a Friend.** Prentice-Hall, 1973.

Risom, Ole. **I Am a Bear.** Western, 1967.

Risom, Ole. **I Am a Mouse.** Western, 1974.

Rockwell, Ann and Harlow. **Toad.** Doubleday, 1972.

Sabin, Francene. **Amazing World of Ants.** Troll-Mar, 1982.

Sabin, Louis. **Amazing World of Butterflies & Moths.** Troll-Mar, 1982.

Selsam, Millicent. **All Kinds of Babies.** Scholastic, 1967.

Selsam, Millicent. **How the Animals Eat.** Hale, 1955.

Selsam, Millicent. **Terry and the Caterpillars.** Harper & Row, 1962.

Showell, Romala. **Learning About Insects and Small Animals.** Wills & Hepworth, 1972.

Garden Walk

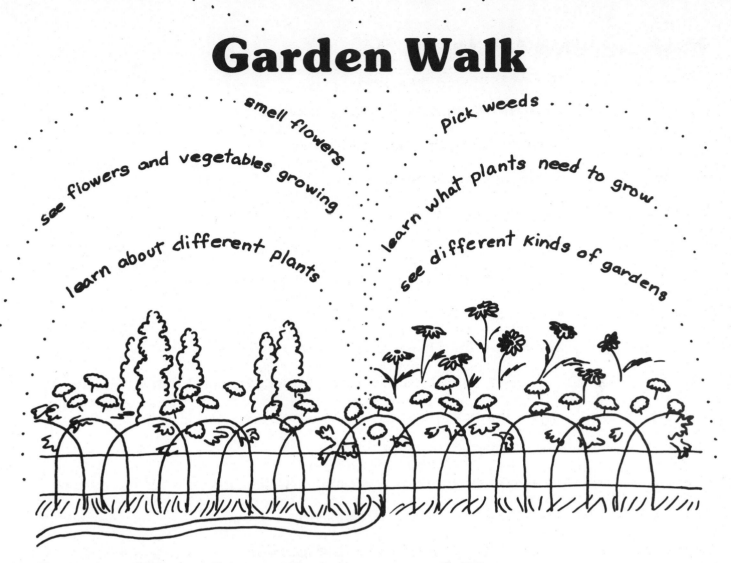

smell flowers . . .

. . . Pick weeds . . .

see flowers and vegetables growing . . .

learn what plants need to grow . . .

learn about different plants . . .

. . . see different kinds of gardens

Some Words to Learn and Use

bulb   seed   plant   leaf   stem   root   flower

blossom   fruit   vegetable   weed   bush   shrub   hoe

rake   trowel   spade   shovel   wheelbarrow   dandelion

grow   bloom   soil   shade   sun   rain   grass   petals

annual   perennial   biennial   bud   sprout   border

climber   gardener   nectar   germinate   seedling

pollinate   stamen   pistil   cutting   hybrid

cross-breeding   rock garden   window box   mulch

fertilizer

Do and Experiment

Bring in some bean seeds, bulbs, grass and flower seeds. Cut some open and show them to the children. Ask the children what would happen if you planted these seeds. Sprinkle some grass seed in dirt and watch it for a few days. Plan to plant the other seeds too and show the children some pictures of plants starting to grow.

Bring in some carrots with plant tops. Cut the top off one carrot and slice it flat so you can put it in a small bowl of water. Watch what happens. Plan to take the other carrots with you on a walk to see if you can find other plants that look like that. Take along some common flowers from your area as well.

Read a Story

Read the story **A Carrot Seed.** Talk about what plants need to grow. Show the children an encyclopedia with pictures of different flowers and gardens.

Talk to Others

Ask friends, neighbors and the children's parents if they garden or if they know of a neighborhood garden your group might visit. Tell the children you have been invited to visit the Jones' garden. (If you can't find one this way, call the garden club, or the agricultural extension service in your community.)

On the Walk / Ideas for Exploring

Observing

As you walk along, notice everything that is blooming and name as many things as you can. This may include shrubs, weeds and trees, as well as garden plants. Bring along a small directory of flowers and plants to help you in the identification process.

Call attention to the setting where things are blooming. Weeds crop up anywhere. Wild flowers may also grow in fields or along the way, whereas gardens will have a more planned look.

Notice the different types of gardens. Do they look formal or informal? Do you see any rock gardens, Japanese gardens, hedges, border gardens, window boxes, hanging baskets, vines or trellises with climbing plants?

Notice the arrangements in gardens. Where are different sized plants placed? Does the garden bed curve? How does it follow the contour of the land? How is the garden area separated from the grass? Are different flowers and plants mixed up or grouped together? Are there differences in flower and vegetable gardens?

Notice the color and appearance of different flowers or plants. Call attention to the parts of the plant. Be sure to tell the children their names, such as stem, leaf, petals, even the pistils and stamens if you can see them. Don't forget to talk about the roots that can't be seen.

Look for other things that may be placed in gardens, such as statues, bird baths, lights, scarecrows, rocks, stones or wood chips. Talk about how they look or what purpose they serve.

Asking

Ask to see the tools that people use in the garden and find out what they are used for. Be sure you get the names of each tool. If possible, have them demonstrated to show how each tool is suited to its task.

Ask what has to be done in the garden regularly to make sure it grows well.

How does the gardener decide where to plant things? Does sun or shade make a difference, or the time of day the bed gets sunshine?

Ask if the children can smell the flowers. Can you take some samples or some plant cuttings back with you?

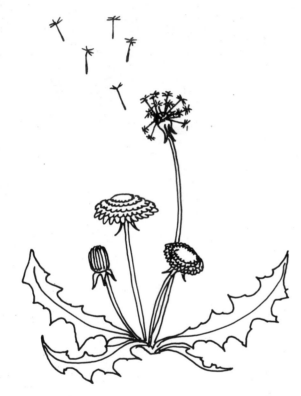

Comparing

Bring along a tape measure and measure the height of some of the different plants. The children can also take hand measures. Measure how far apart the plants are.

Notice similarities and differences among the groups of flowers. Notice that some flowers may be the same except for their colors, or they may vary in size of blossom or height of plant. Talk about families of flowers or hybrid varieties. Do the same thing for vegetables.

Compare the plants or flowers you see growing in the garden to the carrot and flowers you brought along. Do any of them look exactly the same so that you know it is that same flower or a carrot?

Speculating

What might be some problems that would interfere with the plants growing well?

What plants might be hurt by strong winds or bad storms?

What happens to plants if there are too many insects or rabbits in the garden? How do gardeners try to protect their plants? Do you see any fences or scarecrows?

How would the garden look if the plants were put too close together or too far apart or if weeds were not pulled?

How do some plants get started in unusual places where no person planted them? Can bees, birds, and wind be seed carriers?

Collecting

Bring back some samples of wild flowers, all different kinds of seeds or seed pods, and any flowers, vegetables or slips of plants.

Take pictures of the flower and vegetable gardens you see, and planters or any other things of interest related to the walk. If possible, get some pictures of plants in different stages of development, from stems poking through the ground to petals falling off, to the forming of seed pods or berries.

After the Walk / Follow-up Activities

Discussion

Talk about the walk and let the children share the things they remember and like about the walk. Compose a group thank-you note to the person whose garden you visited and include the children's comments and some pictures they might draw.

Review the names of the parts of plants and the specific common flowers and vegetables you saw.

Make up a story about the trip using the pictures you took along the walk. Mount the pictures on individual pages of a small photo album. Write up the children's comments for each picture and mount those with the picture. Invite your host or hostess from the walk to see the finished product.

Make Vegetable Soup

Bring in a variety of fresh vegetables to cut and taste. After tasting some of them raw, cut them up to make soup. Also cut and taste any vegetables you brought back from your walk and add them to the soup. Cook along with any other necessary ingredients to make vegetable soup. Read the folk tale "Stone Soup" before you begin this project. Ask the children if you should put a stone in your soup, too.

Experiments with Seeds

Read the story **Seeds and More Seeds** and try the experiments in that story.

Plant a variety of seeds in different types of environments. Bean seeds sprout very quickly and therefore are good for watching the growth process. Plant seeds in moist paper towels, sponges, dirt, or sand. Place one paper towel and one sponge in pie tins and another set in glass jars with covers. Keep all seed beds moist. Observe which ones need more watering and which ones sprout first. Place the seeds in the towels and sponges in such a way that you can see the seeds and watch them as the roots and plants begin to sprout.

Also plant sweet potatoes. Suspend with the pointed end down in glass jars. Toothpicks poked into the sides of the potatoes will hold them up.

Avocado pits can be planted in much the same way.

Plant some flower bulbs according to the directions.

Table Garden Display

Put your experiments on a special table and add small box gardens planted in flat plastic containers. Fill the medium-sized containers with dirt. In one container sprinkle lots of grass seed. In another, plant different vegetable seeds, sowing the seeds in rows, marking each with the name of the seeds planted. In a third container plant flower seeds in the same way. Keep track of how each garden is doing and write comments about the gardens in a log book kept on the table. Keep a ruler handy to measure things as they grow. When the grass grows fairly tall, let the children cut it with scissors. It will need "cutting" on a regular basis, just as a lawn does.

Life Cycle Chart

Make charts of the life cycles of different plants starting with seeds planted in the ground to the formation of new seed pods. You can make separate charts for flowers and other plants depending on pictures you have. Good sources of pictures for these charts are elementary school workbooks, especially from first or second grade.

Flower Arranging

Look up flower arranging in an encyclopedia and show the children the patterns used to plan flower arrangements. Make some different types of arrangements using the flowers you brought back from the walk. See which ones you like best.

Have the children make a variety of flowers out of egg cartons and pipe cleaners. Have them use the homemade flowers to design their own arrangements. Put styrofoam or some clay or playdough in the bottom of small cans to hold the pipe cleaners in place for their arrangements. Cover the cans to decorate them. Use for table decorations, or send home as gifts.

Flannel Board Flowers and Vegetables

Make several different felt cut-outs of a variety of flowers or vegetables. Use them for counting activities. Give directions such as: plant three tulips in a row, add two yellow daffodils. How many flowers are there? Pick three potatoes from the vegetable garden . . . and so on.

Vegetable Mural

Cut construction paper shapes of vegetables for several common vegetables: carrots, beets, potatoes, squash, cucumbers, tomatoes, peas in pods, broccoli, and so on. On a large sheet of paper draw a line to represent the ground. Paste the vegetables above or below the ground as they would be found when ripe. Add drawings to show what would appear above or below the ground for each plant, such as roots, stems, flowering tops, stalks, vines. Talk about which part of each plant we eat.

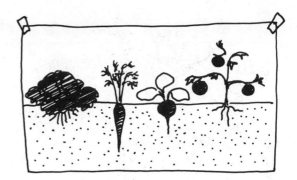

Music and Creative Dramatics

Listen to the record *The Carrot Seed* and act it out.

Have children pretend to be plants growing from tiny seedlings to tall plants.

Act out planting a garden.

Fruit and Vegetable Lotto

Make lotto games using fruit and vegetable seals or pictures from seed catalogs.

Scarecrows

Make a corn cob scarecrow. Use the cob for the head and body and husks for the arms and legs. Dress it in old doll clothes and put it on your garden display table. Talk about why farmers and gardeners use scarecrows. Do they really keep birds and animals away?

Songs, Poems and Fingerplays

In the Garden

To the tune of "Oh My Darling, Clementine"

In the garden, in the garden,
In the garden down the street,
There are flowers, pretty flowers
And they look so nice and neat.

There are roses and petunias
And some lovely daffodils.
There are tulips and begonias
And some lilacs on the hills.

Vary names of flowers if you wish

In the garden, in the garden
That we visit on our street,
Are the flowers, pretty flowers
And their blossoms smell so sweet.

In the garden, in the garden,
In the garden down the street,
We see carrots and some peppers
All in rows that look so neat.

There are green beans and potatoes
And some lovely pumpkin vines.
See the sweet corn and tomatoes,
Vegetables of many kinds.

In the garden, in the garden
That we visit on our street,
See the veggies that will help us
Get the right things when we eat.

Do You See My Garden Grow?

Move hands up to imitate growing

Oh do you see my garden grow,
My garden grow, my garden grow?
Oh do you see my garden grow,
I water it just so.

Pretend to sprinkle garden

Oh do you see my garden grow . . .
I rake it nice and slow.

Oh do you see my garden grow . . .
I weed it, don't you know.

Tulips

One red tulip in the garden grew
Soon a yellow one opened,
Then there were two.

Hold up one finger
Add second finger

Two pretty tulips that we could see,
Now there is a pink one,
And that makes three.

Add third finger

The next morning when I looked out the door
I saw another red one,
And now there are four.

Hold up four fingers

Vegetable Soup *

Choppity Chop, Choppity Chop,
Cut off the bottom,
Cut off the top.

Chop, Chop, Choppity Chop,
What there is left we will
Put in the pot.

*From **Finger Play Fun,** Cleveland Association for the Education of Young Children.

This is the Way

To the tune of "The Mulberry Bush"

This is the way we dig our garden,
Dig our garden, dig our garden.
This is the way we dig our garden,   *Pretend to dig*
So early in the spring.

This is the way we plant the seeds . . .   *Imitate planting*
So early in the morning.

This is the way we water the garden . . .   *Imitate sprinkling*
So early every morning.

This is the way we pull the weeds . . .   *Stoop down and pull weeds*
To let the flowers grow.

And more

Pumpkins and Pumpkin Vines, John the Rabbit, Oats, Peas, Beans and Barley Grow, from **Take a Bite of Music, It's Yummy.** Mary Ann Hall. New England Association for the Education of Young Children, 1982.

Let's Make a Garden, from **Sing A Song.** Roberta MacLaughlin and Lucille Ward. Prentice-Hall, 1960.

Heigh-Ho, Daisies and Buttercups, from **Songs for the Nursery School.** Laura Pendelton MacCarteney. Willis, 1937.

Yellow Daffodil, Mister Carrot, My Garden and many more, from **Finger Frolics.** Liz Cromwell and Dixie Hibner. Partner, 1976.

Pussy Willow, Little Seeds, from **Singing Fun.** Louise Scott and Lucille Wood. Webster, 1954.

Books

Aliki. **A Weed is a Flower—The Life of George Washington Carver.** Prentice-Hall, 1965.

Brown, Marc. **Your First Garden Book.** Litle, Brown, 1981.

Carle, Eric. **The Tiny Seed.** Crowell, 1970.

Carlson, Nancy. **Harriet and the Garden.** Carolrhoda, 1982.

Collier, Ethel. **Who Goes There in My Garden?** Young Scott, 1963.

Fisher, Aileen. **And A Sunflower Grew.** Noble, 1977.

Fisher, Aileen. **Mysteries in the Garden.** Noble, 1977.

Fisher, Aileen. **Petals Yellow and Petals Red.** Noble, 1977.

Fisher, Aileen. **Plant Magic.** Noble, 1977.

Fisher, Aileen. **Seeds on the Go.** Noble, 1977.

Fujikawa, Gyo. **Let's Grow A Garden.** Grosset & Dunlop, 1978.

Golden, Augusta. **Where Does Your Garden Grow?** Crowell, 1967.

Hudlow, Jean. **Eric Plants a Garden.** Whitman, 1971.

Jordan, Helene. **How a Seed Grows.** Crowell, 1960.

Knights, Roger. **The Alphabets in the Garden.** Simon & Schuster, 1982.

Kratz, Marilyn. **The Garden Book.** Denison, 1980.

Kraus, Ruth. **The Carrot Seed.** Harper & Row, 1982.

Lauber, Patricia. **Seeds Pop—Stick—Glide.** Crown, 1981.

Moncure, Jane B. **See My Garden Grow.** Child's World, 1976.

Muntean, Michaela. **A Garden for Miss Mouse.** Parents, 1982.

Rockwell, Anne and Harlow. **How My Garden Grows.** MacMillan, 1982.

Rockwell, Anne and Harlow. **Molly's Woodland Garden.** Doubleday, 1971.

Rockwell, Harlow. **The Compost Heap.** Doubleday, 1974.

Selsam, Millicent and Peterson, Deborah. **The Don't Throw It, Grow it Book of House Plants.** Random House, 1977.

Selsam, Millicent. **The Carrot and Other Root Vegetables.** Morrow, 1971.

Selsam, Millicent. **Seeds and More Seeds.** Harper & Row, 1959.

Selsam, Millicent. **The Plants We Eat.** Morrow, 1955.

Selsam, Millicent. **Vegetables From Stems and Leaves.** Morrow, 1972.

Van Leeuwen, Jean. **Timothy's Flower.** Random House, 1967.

Watson, Aldren. **My Garden Grows.** Viking, 1962.

Weber, Irma E. **Up Above and Down Below.** Addison-Wesley, 1943.

Zokeisha. **My Garden.** Simon & Schuster, 1982.

Zolatov, Charlotte. **In My Garden.** Lothrop, 1960.

House Walk

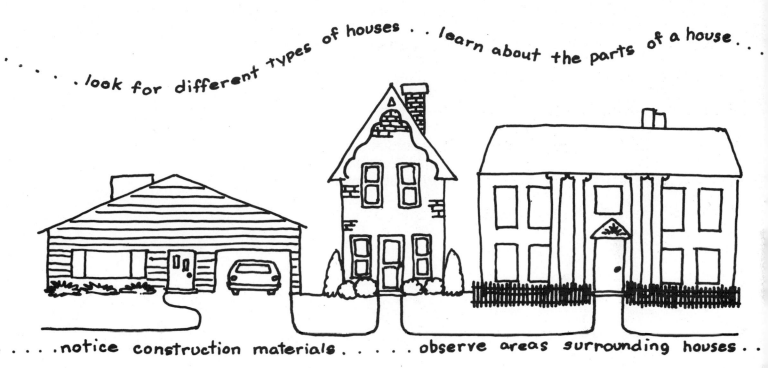

... look for different types of houses . . learn about the parts of a house ...

... notice construction materials . . . . . observe areas surrounding houses ...

Some Words to Learn and Use

apartment building   single-family home   duplex

ranch-type   two-story house   foundation   blueprint

wall   roof   window   door   shutters   chimney   porch

yard   fence   gate   shingle   brick   stucco   stone

wrought iron   concrete blocks   wood   corbelling

doorbell   light   gutter   soffit   TV antenna

clothesline   hose   sprinkler   garden   shrub   sidewalk

blacktop   garage   mailbox   driveway   patio   hedge

Talk About

Have the children tell you about their houses and bring in pictures of their houses or apartments if possible.

Ask children what houses are made of. Ask the children if animals live in houses and why houses are necessary.

Make a Booklet

Make up a booklet telling something about each child's house. There will be lots of things they haven't noticed about their own houses and you might suggest going on a walk to see how the houses nearby are similar to or different from their houses.

On the Walk / Ideas for Exploring

Identifying

Stop in front of several houses and talk about the type of house, the materials it is made of and other distinguishing features. Call attention to several of the words listed above by pointing to examples of them. Have the children tell you the things they notice about each house.

Sing the "Oh, Do You See" song as you walk along and let the children fill in new verses.

Try to walk around some houses to look at the backs to see what they look like.

Comparing

Look for houses made of the same materials or combinations of materials and compare them. Notice similarities and differences in the houses. Some examples: some may be made of wood but different colors, some half stucco and half brick, yellow brick and red brick, and so on.

Talking About

Notice and discuss the placement of chimneys, garages, porches, windows (stained glass, varied shapes, solar, skylights) and any kind of trim (shutters, awnings, "gingerbread," and so on). Talk about whether the houses look like anything special to the children. (Is there one that looks like: a castle, a witch's house, a barn?) Think about what makes them look that way.

Notice the different shapes of roofs and the materials used to make them. Notice how shingles overlap and talk about why roofs are made the way they are. Notice if there are gutters and downspouts around the house and talk about their uses. Where does the water go when it comes out the downspout?

Speculating

Guess about who lives in the house. What clues do you see around the yard or garage to help you guess if there are young children, teenagers, pets, or someone who uses a wheelchair living in a particular house? Can you decide if it's a large or small family? Make up pretend stories about some of the houses in the neighborhood.

Count things related to the house—the number of windows, chimneys, doors, trees around the house.

Guess how many floors are in the house or building. How can you tell? Help the children figure out how to tell the number of floors.

Do you see power lines or telephone lines going into the house? If you don't see them, where could they be? In which houses can they watch TV or cable TV? How can you tell?

After the Walk / Follow-up Activities

Discussion

Talk about the walk. Let the children share their experiences.

Talk about each child's house in more detail. Ask the children what they like best about their houses. Notice any differences from previous discussions. Make additions to the booklet.

Talk about people who work to make our houses. Invite any parents or friends who work in construction, architecture or decorating to come and tell about their work.

Cardboard House

Make houses out of large cartons. Cut windows and doors, then decorate. Make cardboard roofs for the houses. Use a small box to add a chimney. Use small paper or wallpaper squares to cover the roof, overlapping them like the shingles you observed. If you wish, put two boxes together to make a duplex.

Mural

Make a class or group mural of children and their houses. Have children draw pictures of the types of houses they live in, and put children's names over their houses.

Matching Game

Make a real-life matching game using the snapshots the children brought in of their houses. Spread out the pictures on a table or in the middle of a circle. Let a child pick a house picture and try to guess whose house it is. This can be played after the children have told about their own houses and the pictures have been used by the children for a while.

Houses in Other Lands

Look up houses of other lands in a picture encyclopedia. Make a booklet telling about the interesting or unusual ones. Use cut-paper shapes, natural materials and children's drawings to illustrate some of the houses. Bits of grass can be glued on to make thatched roofs; sand or dirt can be sprinkled on glue for mud houses; white squares of construction paper can be pasted on for an igloo, or whipped soap suds can be painted on. Toothpicks could be pasted on for legs and painted brown. Grasscloth, bamboo, brick or other samples from wallpaper books may resemble materials used for houses.

Bulletin Board Match-ups

Set up a bulletin board display matching people, including those from other lands, and types of houses they live in. Use string, yarn, or wire as tie lines to connect those that go together. Make another display matching animals with their habitats.

Rooms in the House

Make a sorting game. Use shoe boxes or large envelopes and put a picture of a household room on each one. Give children magazines or catalogs and let them cut out furniture or other items that go in various rooms. Have them sort the pictures into the appropriate boxes or envelopes.

Flannel Boards

Use felt shapes to make houses on a flannel board. Discuss the parts of a house.

Decorating

Redecorate the housekeeping area. Make pretend wallpaper out of brown packaging paper by printing designs or patterns on the paper or by pasting wallpaper samples to a screen or large cardboard to use in the area. Add curtains or other suitable touches.

Household Activities Pictures or Mural

Have children take the assorted pictures from the "Rooms in the House" activity and use them for an activity picture or mural. Paste the pictures from one room of the house onto a piece of paper and then draw people doing whatever activity gets done in that room (cooking/kitchen; cleaning car/garage; sleeping/bedroom; taking a bath/bathroom).

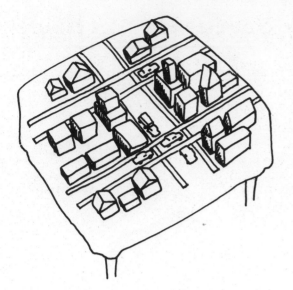

Building

Build houses and garages with unit blocks.

Cover a small table with oilcloth. Make roads with masking tape. Provide a village set or small blocks and cars to set up a neighborhood scene. Let the children create yards around the houses using scrap materials or drawings for fences, bushes, trees, gardens, pools, toys or whatever they wish.

Dramatize

Read the story of the **Three Little Pigs** and have the children dramatize it.

Building Materials Display

Display samples of wood, brick, stucco, shingles and other materials used in building. Talk about the weight and texture of the materials.

Blueprints

Show the children a blueprint. Help them make a blueprint of a dollhouse.

Songs, Poems and Fingerplays

Our House Has Many Rooms

To the tune of "Farmer in the Dell"

Our house has many rooms, our house has
many rooms,
Hi-ho the merry-o, our house has many
rooms.

Our house has a living room,
Our house has a living room,
Hi-ho the merry-o, we sit there you know.

Our house has a bedroom . . .
We sleep there, you know.

Our house has a kitchen . . .
We cook there you know.

To sing as you go walking along; make up verses to describe the things you are seeing

Oh Do You See The ____ House

Oh do you see the apartment house,
The apartment house, the apartment house,
Oh do you see the apartment house,
On the corner of our block?

Oh yes, we see the apartment house
The apartment house, the apartment house,
Oh yes, we see the apartment house,
At the corner of our block.
   (Or)
It's built of wood and rock.

Oh do you see the yellow house . . .
As we walk down the street.
Oh yes, we see the yellow house . . .
It's shutters (mailbox, windows) look so neat.

Oh do you see the stucco house . . .
As we walk down the street?
Oh yes, we see the stucco house . . .
It's flowers look so neat.

Three Houses

A little house, a medium-size house,
And a great big house, I see.

Shall we count them?
Are you ready? 1, 2, 3.

Make small house shape using two hands: join thumbs to form floor, hands form walls, bend fingers to touch each other for roof shape; move hands apart for medium-size house, and way apart for great big house; repeat motions as you say "1, 2, 3"

A Good House

This is the roof of the house so good,
These are the walls that are made of wood.
These are the windows that let in the light,
This is the door that shuts so tight.
This is the chimney so straight and tall,
Oh! What a good house for one and all.

Traditional

Put finger tips together and form roof
Hands straight, with palms facing each other
Join thumbs and join forefingers erect
Clap one hand to other
Put arms up above head.
Repeat first motion

And more

How Many People Live at Your House, from **Singing Fun.** Lucille Wood and Louise Scott, Webster, 1954.

Let's Build a House, from **Sing a Song.** Lucille Wood and Roberta MacLaughlin, Prentice-Hall, 1960.

Books

Arkin, Alan. **Tony's Hard Work Day.** Harper & Row, 1972.

Bannon, Laura. **Best House in the World.** Houghton-Mifflin, 1952.

Burton, Virginia. **Little House.** Houghton-Mifflin, 1942.

Clymer, Eleanor. **Tiny Little House.** Atheneum, 1964.

Cunningham, Alice. **My House.** Concordia, 1973.

De Regniers, Beatrice. **A Little House of Your Own.** Harcourt Brace, 1954.

Green, Mary McBurney. **Everybody Has a House.** Young Scott, 1961.

Harper, Anita. **How We Live.** Harper & Row, 1977.

Krauss, Ruth. **Very Special House.** Harper & Row, 1953.

Kunhardt, Edith. **Martha's House.** Western, 1982.

Le Sieg, Theodore. **In a People House.** Random, 1972.

Lewis, Ellis, M. **The Snug Little House.** Atheneum, 1981.

Lionni, Leo. **Biggest House in the World.** Pantheon, 1968.

Manley, Deborah. **A New House.** Raintree, 1979.

My House. Western, 1978.

My Yard. Western, 1978.

Oppenheim, Joanne. **Have You Seen Houses.** Addison-Wesley, 1973.

Sandberg, Inger. **Boy With Many Houses.** Delacorte, 1970.

Scarry, Richard. **My House.** Western, 1976.

Shapp, Martha and Charles. **Let's Find Out About Houses.** Watts, 1975.

Skorpen, Liesel. **We Were Tired of Living in a House.** Coward, 1969.

The Three Little Pigs. (Traditional.) Illustrator: Garth Williams. Golden, 1958.

Youldon, Gillian. **Homes.** Watts, 1982.

Zokeiska. **My House.** Simon & Schuster, 1982.

48

Shadow Walk

learn what causes them . . . . .

see how they change . . . .

observe shadows . . .

experiment with shadows . . .

Some Words to Learn and Use

shadow   light   dark   reflection   angle   sunshine

shade   silhouette   shadow picture   shadow play

sundial   eclipse   opaque   hazy   diffuse   direct   cast

shape   size   oblique   elongated   projector

Before the Walk / Introductory Activities

Read

Read Robert Louis Stevenson's poem "My Shadow" to the children. Ask them if they know what a shadow is and if they have noticed their own shadows. What do they think causes shadows? Why did the boy in the poem say his shadow was lazy and still in bed?

Demonstrate

Bring in a doll, a water glass and a flashlight to demonstrate how shadows are produced. Stand the doll up on a table and shine the flashlight at it so the light comes from one side. This should cast a shadow on the opposite side. Explain that because the doll is an opaque object and doesn't let the light shine through it, a dark outline of the object is passed on by the light and makes a shadow of the object.

Shine the light on the empty water glass and see what happens. The light passes right through the glass so it shouldn't leave any outline of its shape. Move the flashlight around so that it shines at different angles on the doll. Move it so it is closer to the doll and further away from the doll. Does that make any change in the shadow? If you wish, measure the shadow as it is cast from different angles and write up your findings. Plan to go outside at different times of day to look for and measure shadows.

Peter pan loses his shadow

50

On the Walk / Ideas for Exploring

Observing

On a sunny day, look for shadows as you walk along. Notice the shadows of cars, trees, houses, street signs, people, animals and anything else you can find. Plan to look for shadows in the morning and again in the afternoon to see if they look different.

Let the children observe their own and each other's shadows. Can they make their shadows move or do things? Observe what happens. Sing one of the shadow songs and imitate its actions. Make different shapes of the shadows by moving arms and legs or by sitting down.

Look for shadows from clouds, airplanes, kites, balloons, clothes hanging on lines. If you see some shaded areas in the yard or street, try to figure out what is producing that shade.

Are the shadows the same on both sides of the street? Are there places where there aren't any shadows? Do moving things also have shadows? Do you see shadows from moving cars, running animals or other things? What do you notice about the shadows as they move?

Experimenting

Trace around the children's shadows in the morning. Mark where their feet were placed so they can stand in the same spot again later in the day to see what happens to their shadows. Measure their shadows each time to see how they change. When are their shadows the longest and the shortest? Test frequently throughout the day to see how it changes. Write down the length after each measurement. Are their shadows in the same places each time or do they move? Make little lines to show where their shadows are each time.

Take along a thermometer to measure the temperature in the sun and in the shade. Talk about the difference and note why it feels cooler in the shade.

Measure the size of shadows from other things such as parked cars, signs, fire hydrants, trees and so on. Measure with tape measures or by pacing. Keep track of the size of those shadows. Measure them at other times of the day to see if they change also.

Take some pictures and try to get the shadows in the pictures.

Go out on a cloudy, hazy day to see if you can find any shadows.

Playing Games

Play games with the shadows such as running and standing in someone else's shadow, tagging shadows, catching shadows in hoops and so on.

Play shadow tag designating the large shadows of buildings or trees as "safe" zones.

Play "Don't Step On My Shadow" tag. The child chosen to become "It" tries to step on the shadow of another child who then becomes "It." Play this game in a large open area to avoid children bumping into things.

After the Walk / Follow-up Activities

Discussion

Talk about your observations of shadows. Write a story about those observations trying to make some generalizations about shadows. Examples: shadows are longest late in the afternoon and shortest in the middle of the day, and there are no shadows when it is cloudy. How do these observations compare to those of the doll's shadow done before the walk? Think about how the size of the shadow may be related to the position of the light in relation to the object.

Look for magazine pictures that have shadows in them and bring them in to discuss. Wonder where the light would be to make the shadows fall as they do.

Talk about the word "eclipse" and explain that it occurs when one celestial body comes between another body and the sun, blocking light and producing a shadow. An eclipse of the moon occurs when the earth happens to come between the moon and the sun, producing a shadow of the earth on the moon. Demonstrate this with a flashlight and two balls in a darkened room.

Make a Sundial

Insert a pencil or dowel into the center of a paper plate and then into a small container of clay so that the pencil will stand erect with the plate at its base. Place in a sunny window. Look at it every hour during the day and draw a line of the shadow of the pencil on the plate each time. Think about what the finished picture looks like. Discuss how ancient civilizations used the sun to tell time.

Drawing Shadows

Have the children draw pictures of trees, houses, cars, and so forth on a mural, leaving lots of room between each item. Then have the children make shadows of the things in the mural. Are the shadows all going to be going in the same direction?

Homework with Shadows

Read the story **What Makes a Shadow** and try out some of the experiments suggested in it. Have the children try making shadows at night at home, telling about what they noticed the next day. It might be a good idea to let parents know you have suggested that, so they can help find a good light source and a wall or counter surface. Also, ask the children to notice shadows in their houses at night. Are there shadows of furniture, plants, railings, doors and so on? Perhaps the children can make pictures of the things that made shadows in their houses. Or their parents can write some things down to help them remember.

Pretending

Divide the children into pairs. Let one child be the shadow, doing whatever the other child does. They can try all kinds of actions with the shadow following exactly the movements of the leader. Have the children change positions so they both have turns to be initiators and shadows.

Shadow Pictures

Bring in an overhead projector or any type of projector. Turn on so light shines on one wall. Let the children make all kinds of shadow pictures with their hands. Hold objects in front of the light to see what shadows they project.

Mount some large sheets of white paper on the wall and let the children trace around the shadows with markers. To make silhouette pictures of the children, have them stand sideways between the light and the paper mounted on the wall. Trace around the profile projected onto the paper. Cut out and mount on a larger piece of paper or tagboard (a very nice gift idea).

Shadow Plays

Hang up a white sheet and place a projector behind it. Have a few children stand between the light and the sheet. Let the others stay on the opposite side of the sheet to see what happens. Have the performers box in the air toward each other to see what it looks like on the other side of the sheet. Hold up objects behind the sheet and see if the children can guess what they are from their shadows. Have a child perform an action, such as eating, waving, pretending to sew, to see if the other children can guess what the performer is doing.

Make Colored Shadows

Bring in two flashlights and cover them with different colored cellophane such as colored candy wrappers. Hold some small objects up in front of the white paper on the wall. Shine the light on the object and see what color shadow it makes.

Songs, Poems and Fingerplays

Five Men All in a Row

See the five men all in a row	*Hold up five fingers*
See their shadows facing just so	*Hold second hand parallel to first*
The first one bends and says "How do"	*Bend thumb*
And then its shadow does so too.	*Bend second thumb*
The next one starts to twirl around	*Twirl finger on first hand*
And so does its shadow without a sound.	*Corresponding finger does same*
Whatever the first man tried to do	*Fingers on first hand make different motions*
The second one said "I'll do the same as you."	*Fingers on second hand repeat motions*

(This can also be done with pairs of children, one doing the motions initially and the other following exactly.)

To the tune of "Oh Dear, What Can the Matter Be?"

Oh Dear, Where Can My Shadow Be?

Oh dear, where can my shadow be,
Oh dear, where can my shadow be,
Oh dear, where can my shadow be,
When the sun's high in the sky?

It's lost, lost, lost at the foot of me,
Lost, lost, lost at the foot of me,
Oh dear, lost at the foot of me,
'Cuz the sun's high overhead.

Oh dear, where can my shadow be,
Oh dear, where can my shadow be,
Oh dear, where can my shadow be,
When the sun hides in the clouds?

It's gone, gone, gone far away from me,
Gone, gone, gone far away from me,
Oh dear, gone far away from me,
'Cuz the sun hides in the clouds.

Oh, Do You See My Shadow Go

Oh do you see my shadow go,
My shadow go, my shadow go.

Oh do you see my shadow go,
It goes along with me.

Oh do you see my shadow bend,
My shadow bend, my shadow bend.

Oh do you see my shadow bend,
It bends along with me.

Additional verses:

Oh do you see my shadow wave . . .
Oh do you see my shadow jump . . .
Oh do you see my shadow stretch . . .
Oh do you see my shadow hop . . .

To the tune of "The Muffin Man"

Children walk along

Children bend

Children imitate appropriate motions

Books

Branley, Franklyn M. **Eclipse: Darkness in Daytime.** Crowell, 1973.

Bulla, Clyde. **What Makes A Shadow.** Harper & Row, 1962.

DeRegniers, Beatrice and Isabel Gordon. **The Shadow Book.** Harcourt, 1960.

Gomi, Tara. **Shadows.** Heion International, 1981.

Goor, Ron and Nancy. **Shadows Here, There and Everywhere.** Crowell, 1981.

Mahy, Margaret. **The Boy With Two Shadows.** Watts, 1971.

Schneider, Herman and Nina. **Science Fun With a Flashlight.** McGraw-Hill, 1975.

Tree Walk

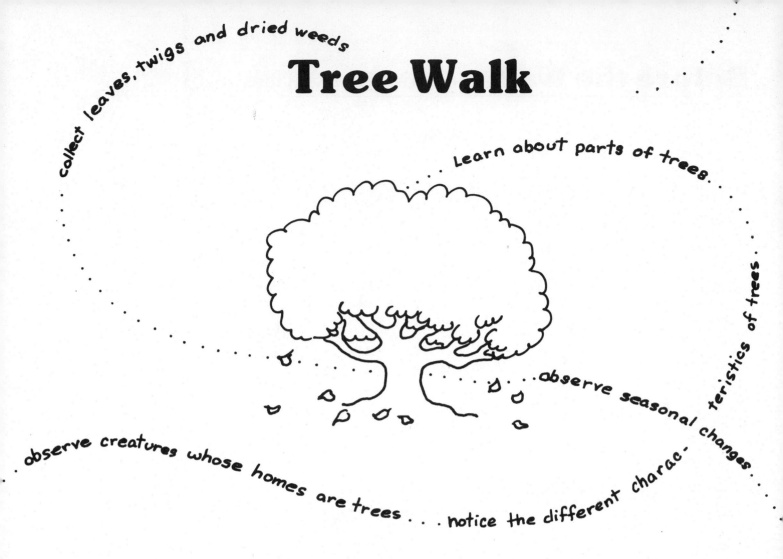

collect leaves, twigs and dried weeds

Learn about parts of trees.

observe seasonal changes

notice the different charac-teristics of trees

observe creatures whose homes are trees

Some Words to Learn and Use

leaf   trunk   shade   bark   branch   crown   twig

bud   acorn   seeds   nuts   fruit   berries   roots

deciduous   coniferous   evergreen   birch   maple   oak

pine   palm   elm   poplar   spruce   needles

pine cones   wood   broadleaf   needleleaf   log   timber

lumberjack   forest   orchard   sapling

Before the Walk / Introductory Activities

Display

Put leaves, nuts, acorns and berries on a low table along with a magnifying glass and some books about trees. Ask the children questions about some of the items. Let the children look at pictures of trees in the books.

Talk About

To stimulate discussion, use the pictures from books or magazine pictures of different kinds of trees at different seasons of the year: Do trees look like this now? Do we have trees like this near us? Shall we go look?

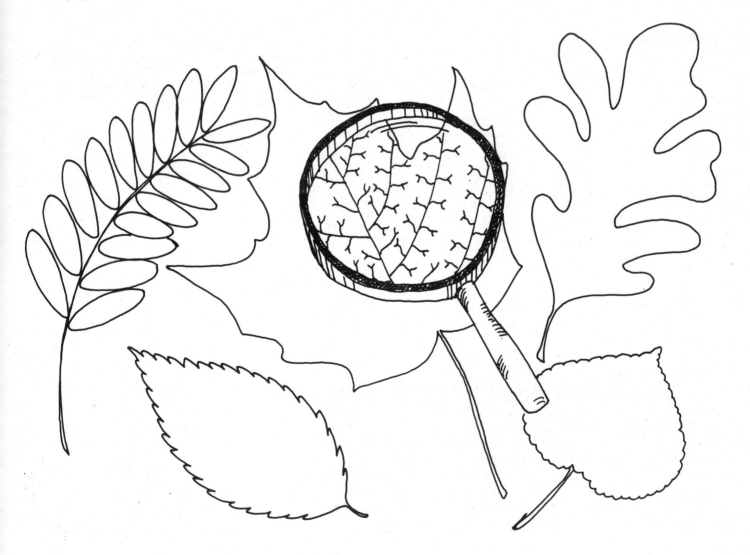

On the Walk / Ideas for Exploring

Identifying
Take along a picture book with good clear pictures of trees, leaves and bark to help identify the trees you see on the walk. The T volume of an encyclopedia, a paperback book of trees, or catalogs from local nurseries might be some sources for pictures to use.

Keep a list of the common trees you are able to identify. If you wish, collect some leaves or bark samples from the unknown trees so they can be checked on later. To help you remember the ones you have identified, you might tape a leaf next to the name on your list. Things you'll need to take on this walk are tree book, pencil, tape, scratch paper and a bag to collect things.

Collecting
Have the children bring along some bags to collect lots of nuts, seeds, cones and leaves to use for later projects—either identification activities, or art activities. (See "After the Walk" section.) You might wish to collect and label some master samples of your own so you'll be able to help sort out and identify items in the children's collections later on.

Observing
Notice the shade around some trees. Decide which trees would be good for climbing, or for sitting under.

Look for unusual things about the trees: split trunks or branches, strange formations, trees that bend in one direction. Wonder about what caused these things.

Look for signs of animal life around trees. Are there birds, birds' nests, squirrels, or insects using the trees? Watch quietly and see if you can see any signs of life in the trees. Listen for sounds of birds singing or pecking at trees or squirrels running up and down trees.

Speculating
Look for things that are edible from trees and things that are nonedible (or even poisonous). What things do animals or birds eat from trees?

Notice the trunks of large trees and the heavy root structure going into the ground. Guess how far the roots of the tree may go and make a circle around the tree to show how far the roots may extend. Can you see any roots for the small trees? The root systems go 15 feet or more under the ground and spread out to take up as

much room under the ground as the branches and leaves (the crown of the tree) take up above the ground. Talk about what the roots do for the tree. Do roots of trees ever cause problems? What kinds? Make some guesses about roots of big and little trees. Why are some very little trees supported by stakes and ropes?

Comparing

Stop and examine very carefully several different trees. Look at size, shape, color, and texture. Notice the trunk, the bark, the leaf structure, and name those parts of the tree. Talk about the differences in the trees. Call the children's attention to the difference between evergreen trees and deciduous trees in terms of structure, texture, and color. Pick a favorite example of each kind and plan to visit them frequently during the year to watch what happens to them in the way of changes (bearing fruit, shedding leaves, new growth, and so on).

Take some tape measures along and measure around some of the trunks. Children can also measure with their arms; some very big trees will need two children to reach around them.

Sensing

Examine the trees in multi-sensory ways. Huddle up close to the trunk of the tree and look up at the sky through the branches. Feel all the textures of the trees. Close your eyes and listen to the trees. Can you hear them? What can you tell about them? Look at trees from the distance as well, to take in the whole effect.

Take along some crayons and paper and make rubbings of the bark—and/or have the children make simple drawings of the trees.

Talking About

Encourage the children to describe how the trees look to them and the things about the trees that especially interest them. Which trees look the prettiest to them? As the year goes along, continue that discussion and decide when trees look the prettiest or the most interesting. Talk about what happens to the trees at each season.

Make some generalizations about some of the trees you've seen related to size, branch structure, and so on. Some examples might be: Evergreen trees have branches that start right at the ground while other trees branch high up off the ground. New trees have very small trunks; older trees have thick trunks.

After the Walk / Follow-up Activities

Discussion

Talk about the walk. Let the children share their experiences.

Write a short story about what the children saw on the walk.

Let the children dramatize the growth of a tree from a seedling in the ground to a tall tree. Talk about what trees need to grow.

Sponge Painting

Have children make sponge painting pictures of trees. Trace around the child's arm and hand to form the trunk and branches. Color with brown crayon or chalk. Set out small containers of yellow, red, orange and green paint. Cut sponges into small pieces. Using clothespins as handles for the sponges, have children dip them into paint and then press lightly on paper around trunks and branches to produce the effect of colorful leaves.

Seasonal Mural

Make seasonal murals using trees and the appropriate creatures found in trees in each season. Show how the trees and their foliage look during each season. Add birds' nests to the trees in spring, bugs in summer and squirrels in the fall. Be sure to include evergreen trees in each season. Murals can be expanded to include diverse sections of the country where trees may look different—palm trees in the south, evergreen trees in the north or mountain areas, and so on.

Trees and Leaves Matching Chart

Make a large mural, bulletin board or a chart on posterboard to match trees with their leaves and fruits/nuts/seeds. Colorful yarn or telephone wire can be used as tie-lines to connect the trees with the appropriate leaves. You can use items collected on walks or collect pictures of trees and leaves from magazines and books. Examples for mural or chart:

Oak Tree—Oak Leaves—Acorns
Pine Tree—Pine Needles—Pine Cones
Apple Tree—Leaves and Blossoms—Apple
Cottonwood Tree—Leaves—Cotton Fluff
(Use types of trees found in your neighborhood.)

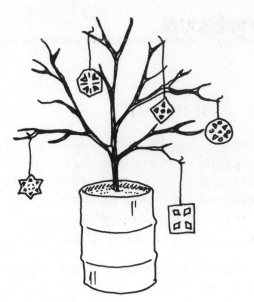

Tree Products

Discuss tree products such as timber, paper, toothpicks. Discover items in the room that are tree products. Look up trees in an encyclopedia and look at pictures of trees and their products. Set up a display area featuring trees and their products; collect different samples of bark, wood scraps and small items made from wood.

A Tree for all Seasons

Bring in a large branch of a tree. Place in a coffee can of sand. In the fall make colored leaves to hang on the branches. In the winter hang paper snowflakes on the tree. Other seasonal items can be hung from the tree branch as well (pumpkins, mittens, valentine hearts, and so on).

Torn Paper Trees

Provide cut paper trunks and branches to make tree pictures. Let the children tear paper scraps for leaves and glue onto paper. If you wish, add roots using scraps of paper and string.

Apple Trees

Make a before-and-after picture of apple trees. For the before picture use cotton or tissue paper to represent the apple blossoms. For the after picture have the children make red thumbprint apples using a red ink pad to color their thumbs. Be sure to observe apple trees in spring and fall.

For the Birds

Make a bird's nesting ball to hang on a tree in the spring and a bird feeder in the fall. For the nesting ball put bits and pieces of yarn, ribbon, or string in a piece of netting cut from an onion bag. Tie and hang near a tree. Watch the birds pick at the contents.

For a bird feeder, roll a large pine cone in peanut butter and dip in bird seed. Hang on a tree you can readily observe.

Leaf Rubbings

Make leaf rubbings by placing a piece of paper over a leaf. Rub the paper with the side of a crayon.

Collages

Make a collage of twigs, nuts, leaves, and other treasures found on the walk.

Songs, Poems and Fingerplays

To the tune of "Oh, Christmas Tree"

Oh, Maple Tree

Oh, maple tree, oh maple tree,
How pretty are your branches.
Your pointed leaves are colored bright,
All red and gold in the sunlight.
Oh, maple tree, oh maple tree,
How pretty are your branches.

Oh, evergreen tree, oh evergreen tree,
How lovely are your branches.
Your many needles, soft and fine,
Your special cones and scent of pine.
Oh, evergreen tree, oh evergreen tree,
How lovely are your branches.

Traditional

Fall

The leaves are green, the nuts are brown,
They hang so high, they'll never come down.
But leave them alone 'til the bright fall weather,
And then they will all come down together.

Traditional

Apple Tree

Point with one hand

Way up high in the apple tree,
Two little apples smiled at me.

Pretend to shake tree

I shook that tree as hard as I could,
And down came those apples,

Rub tummy

Mmm they were good.

The Little Squirrel

Traditional

The little squirrel with a bushy tail,
Goes scampering all around.

And everyday he stores away,
The nuts that he has found.

The Squirrel

Traditional

Whiskey, friskey, hippety-hop,
Up he goes to the tree top.

Whirley, twirley, round and round,
Down he scampers to the ground.

Point to eye and then in outward direction
Make a large overhead circular motion with arms

Extend two arms upward overhead

Jump as if to touch ceiling

The Big Tree

I see a tree,
It looks mighty
Big to me.

It's branches are
So very high,
It almost seems to
Touch the sky.

Traditional

Riddle

First it was a pretty flower,
Dressed in pink and white.
Then it was a tiny ball,
Almost hid from sight.

Round and green and large it grew,
Then it turned to red.
It will make a splendid pie,
For your Thanksgiving spread.

Answer: apple

Traditional

Fall

Fall has come again,
And on each flower and weed,
Where little blossoms used to grow,
I found a pod of seed.

And more

Falling Leaves, I Am a Pine Tree, Springtime, from **Singing Fun.** Lucille Wood and Louise Scott, Webster, 1954.

Falling Leaves, The Month is October, Autumn, Shake the Apple Tree, from **Songs for the Nursery School.** Laura Pendleton MacCarteney. Willis, 1937.

Books

Brandt, Keith. **Discovering Trees.** Troll, 1982.

Bulla, Clyde R. **A Tree is a Plant.** Crowell, 1960.

Carrick, Donald. **The Tree.** MacMillan, 1971.

Day, Jennifer W. **What is a Tree?** Western, 1975.

Ernst, Kathryn. **Mr. Tamarin's Trees.** Crown, 1976.

Fisher, Aileen. **As the Leaves Fall Down.** Noble, 1977.

Fisher, Aileen. **A Tree With A Thousand Uses.** Noble, 1977.

Kirkpatrick, Rena K. **Look at Trees.** Raintree, 1978.

Nikly, Michelle. **The Emperor's Plum Tree.** Morrow, 1982.

Oppenheim, Joanne. **Have You Seen Trees?** Addison-Wesley, 1967.

Podendorf, Illa. **Trees (New True Book of).** Childrens Press, 1982.

Silverstein, Shel. **The Giving Tree.** Harper & Row, 1964.

Simon, Seymour. **A Tree on Your Street.** Holiday, 1973.

Tresselt, Alvin. **Johnny Maple Leaf.** Lothrop, 1948.

Tresselt, Alvin. **The Dead Tree.** Parents, 1972.

Udry, Janice. **A Tree is Nice.** Harper & Row, 1956.

Winter, Ginny L. **What's in My Tree?** Astor-Honor, 1962.

Truck Walk

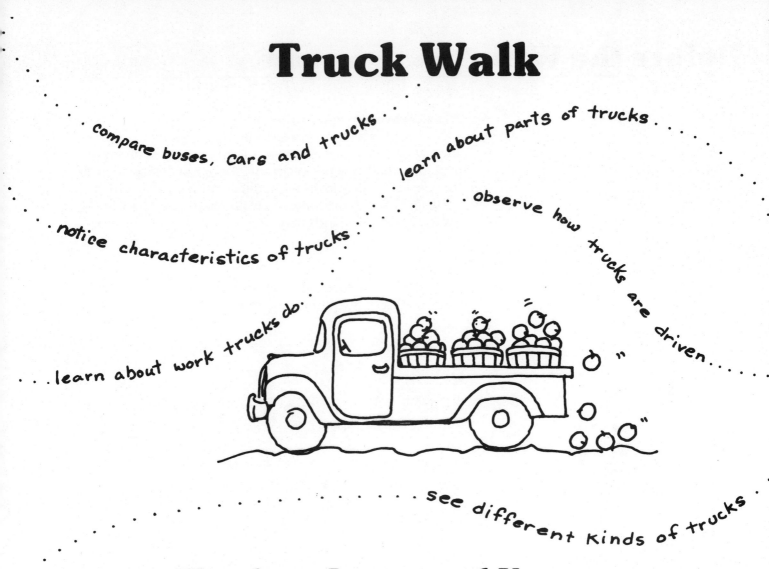

...compare buses, cars and trucks...

...learn about parts of trucks...

...notice characteristics of trucks...

...observe how trucks are driven...

...learn about work trucks do...

...see different kinds of trucks...

Some Words to Learn and Use

tow truck   dump truck   cement mixer   steam shovel

crane   derrick   car carrier   panel truck   semi-trailer

refrigerator truck   caterpillar truck   tank truck

livestock truck   sanitation truck   pick-up truck

moving van   fire truck   delivery truck   wheels   chassis

gasoline   diesel oil   engine   motor   body   cab

truck driver   bookmobile   bus

Before the Walk / Introductory Activities

Talk About

Display picture books about trucks along with model trucks or toy trucks. Ask the children how cars and trucks are different. Ask the children if there are different kinds of trucks. What makes them different? Suggest going for a walk to see if there are any trucks in the neighborhood and to see what kinds they are.

List

Let the children tell you all they know about trucks. Make a list of the things they mention.

On the Walk / Ideas for Exploring

Identify

Find a truck that is parked and examine it very closely, noticing the way the truck is put together.

Take along a picture book with names and pictures of the parts of trucks so you can identify them and compare the pictures to the real thing.

Make a list of all the different trucks or larger vehicles you see. Point out the names of as many types of trucks as you can. Make notes of the ones with which the children are most familiar and the ones about which they want to learn more.

Comparing

Observe the differences between trucks that are in one piece: smaller mail trucks, delivery vans, pick-ups, as opposed to those that come in two parts: cabs and trailers.

Count the number of wheels on different trucks. Are the tires the same size on all types of trucks?

Compare cars and trucks. In what ways are they alike and how are they different? Look for specific parts that each might have. Notice their similarities and differences: gas tanks, mirrors, windows, seats, tires, and so on.

Listen to the sounds trucks make as they go by. Compare the sounds of trucks and cars. What can you tell from the sounds?

Observing

Notice how different trucks are driven. Where does the driver sit? Observe any differences about where the driver sits in a car compared to other vehicles (buses, large trucks, vans).

If possible, have a driver show the children the inside parts of the driving area of a vehicle. Ask the child questions about the vehicle and how it is driven, as well as inquiring about other special features of that vehicle.

Speculating

Wonder what type of loads the trucks are carrying. What clues do you have about what work the truck does? How is it suited to the work it does? What parts does it need for its job? Could a mail truck tow a car?

How might it feel to drive a truck? What are some problems the driver could have in your neighborhood?

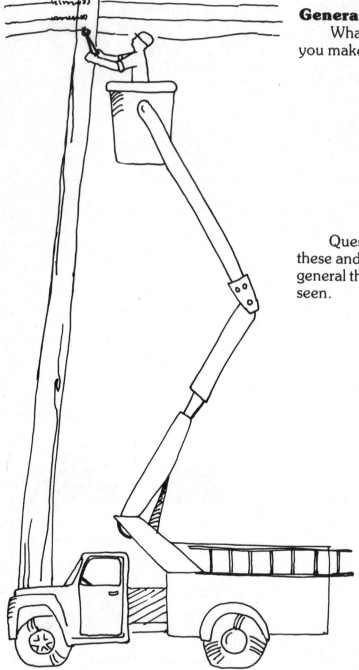

Can trucks go backwards? How can they see? What happens with trucks that have trailers when they need to go backwards? Do you hear a ringing noise like a bell made by some trucks when they begin to go in reverse (a warning to those around that the truck is backing up)? Can big trucks get gas nearby?

Think about why some trucks have more wheels than others.

Wonder if just anyone can drive a truck. Would you need to know special things? What about the driver's license?

Generalizing

What kinds of general statements about trucks can you make on your return walk? Some samples might be:

- Trailer trucks have many more wheels.
- Trucks that carry heavy loads need more wheels.
- Trucks have very large gas tanks.
- Big trucks are hard to back up and need a lot of room to turn.
- Drivers need to be way up high to see the road well and judge distances.
- Big trucks and buses have big steering wheels.

Questions you ask might help the children think of these and others. Try to get the children to tell some general things they've noticed about the trucks they've seen.

After the Walk / Follow-up Activities

Discussion

Talk about the walk. Let the children share their experiences.

Discuss the uses we make of trucks and set up a transportation bulletin board showing some trucks, the products they carry and the places they take those products (example: a car carrier taking cars to a new car dealership). With older children, discuss role of trucks as part of our transportation system. Some sample questions might be: How do people transport big items (furniture, refrigerators) from stores to home, or from their home to a new house when they move? How does gasoline get into the tanks and pumps at the service station? How does the farmer get the things he grows to the market? What other things do trucks carry from factory to store?

Invite a truck driver to visit your group, preferably *with* truck. One source would be service or delivery trucks in your area. If possible let children, a few at a time, climb up into the cab section of the truck. Write a story about the visit and the truck. Be sure to include what it feels like to be way up in the cab. Talk about the work the truck driver does. Ask the child how a tire gets changed.

Dramatic Play

Use toy trucks to carry blocks. Build roads for different types of trucks.

Use dump trucks and tractors and tow trucks in the sandbox, making roads for them.

Mural

Have the children find pictures of different kinds of trucks. Paste them on a long sheet of paper for a truck mural. Discuss what each truck does.

Truck Lotto

Make some homemade games about trucks. A lotto game can be made using pictures of real or toy trucks from catalog or magazines, or truck seals available in school supply or gift shops may be used. Make three or four master boards with four to six pictures of trucks on each one. Mount a duplicate picture of each truck on a small card to use to match those on the master board. A Tonka Toy Co. catalog or brochure is one good source for pictures of trucks. Remember you need two identical pictures of each truck.

Our Big Book of Trucks

Make a book of trucks using magazine pictures. Be sure to include pictures of different parts of trucks and write in the names of those various parts. Write up and include other information children tell you about each truck. Notice how much they've learned.

Cardboard Box Trucks

Make a variety of trucks out of cardboard boxes. Children can pretend to drive them and deliver whatever comes in that truck.

Transportation Match-up

Make a transportation matching game. Children match the pictures of products or items to be transported to the picture of the type of truck that would be used. Again select samples from magazines or catalogs. Some suggestions for the game are:

        Boats or cars—Boat or car carrier
        Fruits, vegetables—Pick-up truck
        Milk—Refrigerated tanker
        Cement—Cement mixer
        Parcels—UPS truck
        Furniture—Moving van

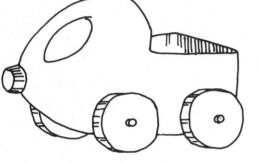

Bleach Bottle Trucks

Cut large plastic bleach bottle and decorate it to resemble a truck. Attach wooden wheels with dowels so they turn. Attach wire, string or telephone cord to pull the truck.

Woodworking

Let the children make trucks out of scrap wood to use in play.

Cut Paper Trucks

Cut different shapes out of construction paper. Let the children paste them together to make a variety of trucks. Attach circles for wheels using brass fasteners.

Truck Repair Shop

Set up a truck repair shop or a truck service station for all the trucks you have.

Songs, Poems and Fingerplays

To the tune of "Mary Wore a Red Dress"

Drove a Truck

Tommy drove a dump truck, dump truck, dump truck,
Tommy drove a dump truck, all day long.
Susie drove a tow truck, tow truck, tow truck,
Susie drove a tow truck, all day long.

*(Continue the song using all the children's
names and several different trucks; let the
children choose the type of truck they wish to drive)*

Old MacDonald Had a Truck

To the tune of "Old MacDonald Had a Farm"

Old MacDonald had a truck, E-I-E-I-O
And on his truck he had a horn, E-I-E-I-O.

With a "beep-beep" here and a "beep-beep" there,
Here a "beep," there a "beep," everywhere a "beep-beep,"
Old MacDonald drove his truck, E-I-E-I-O.

Additional verses:

Wheels, with a "whrr-whrr"
Windshield wipers, with a "swish-swish"
Brakes, with a "screech-screech"
Radio, with a "rock 'n roll"

*Hold up five fingers; lower one finger as each truck
drives away;*

>   or

*Have five children hold pictures of trucks named in
the verse; as each truck drives away, that child sits
down*

Five Big Trucks

Five big trucks outside our door,
The dump truck drove away,
Then there were four.
Four big trucks that I can see,
The garbage truck drove away,
Then there were three.
Three big trucks with work to do,
The moving van drove on,
Then there were two.
Two big trucks shining in the sun,
The milk truck pulled away,
And then there was one.
One mail truck whose work was all done,
Pulled away and then there were none.

Books

Alexander, Anne. **ABC of Cars and Trucks.** Doubleday, 1971.

Alvera. **The Tiny Little Tow Truck.** Exposition, 1980.

Burton, Virginia. **Katy and the Big Snow.** Houghton-Mifflin, 1943.

Cameron, Elizabeth. **The Big Book of Real Trucks.** Grosset & Dunlop, 1970.

Cave, J. Ronald. **Trucks.** Watts, 1982.

Dugan, William. **The Truck and Bus Book.** Western, 1966.

Gibbons, Gail. **Trucks.** Harper & Row, 1981.

Greene, Carla. **Truck Drivers: What Do They Do?** Harper & Row, 1967.

Holl, Adelaide. **ABC Book of Cars, Trucks and Machines.** McGraw-Hill, 1970.

Karen, Edward. **Behind the Wheel.** Holt Rinehart, 1972.

Kesselman, Judi R. and Franklyn Peterson. **Vans.** Dandelion, 1979.

Mathieu, Joseph. **Big Joe's Trailer Truck.** Random House, 1974.

McNaught, Harry. **Trucks.** Random House, 1976.

McNaught, Harry. **The Truck Book.** Random House, 1978.

Miryam. **The Happy Man and His Dump Truck.** Western, 1982.

Penick, Ib. **The Pop-Up Book of Trucks.** Random House, 1974.

Petrie, Catherine. **Joshua James Likes Trucks.** Childrens Press, 1982.

Piper, Watty. **Watty Piper's Trucks.** Platt & Munk, 1978.

Richards, Norman and Pat. **Trucks and Super Trucks.** Doubleday, 1980.

Scarry, Richard. **Great Big Car and Truck Book.** Western, 1951.

Scarry, Richard. **Cars and Trucks and Things That Go.** Western, 1974.

Schultz, Charles M. **Snoopy's Facts and Fun Book About Trucks.** Random House, 1980.

Witty, Susan. **Truck Book.** Western, 1969.

Wolfe, Robert. **The Truck Book.** Carolrhoda, 1981.

Young, Miriam Burt. **If I Drove a Truck.** Lothrop, 1967.

Windy Day Walk

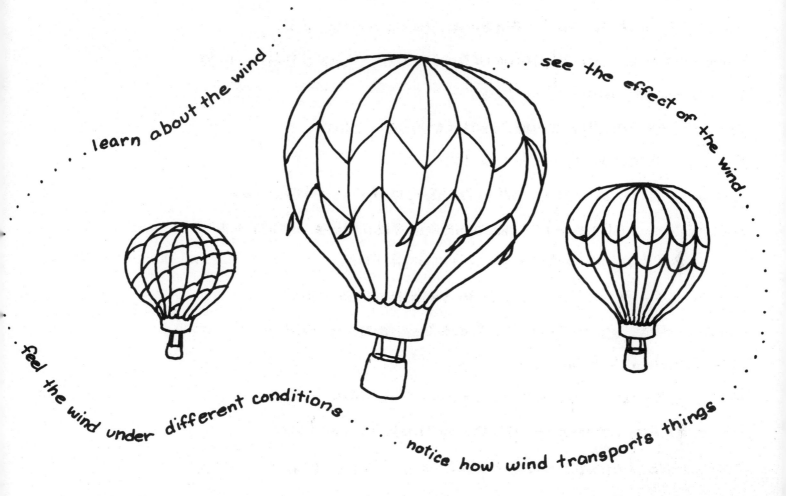

learn about the wind

see the effect of the wind.

feel the wind under different conditions . . . .

notice how wind transports things

Some Words to Learn and Use

blowing   breeze   gale   calm   becalmed   tornado

hurricane   whirl   whirlwind   prevailing   knots

velocity   weathervane   direction   anemometer

wind speed   wind chill   meteorologist   pressure   high

low   gust   windmill

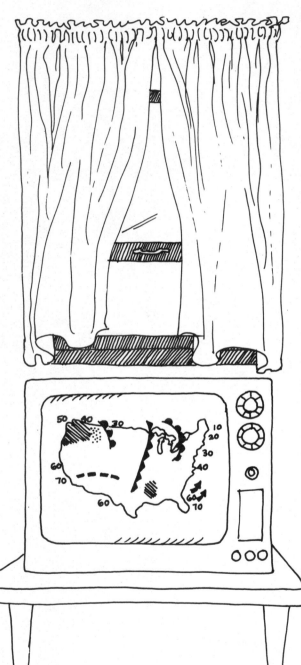

Talk About

Ask the children if they have watched the weather report on TV. Talk about the things the weather report always mentions, such as storm fronts moving in, high or low pressure areas, and so forth. Ask the children what makes the storm fronts move and how the meteorologists can predict some types of weather. Ask the children if they have heard the weather man talk about the wind and what is usually said about it. Do they mention the direction the wind comes from and how fast it is moving? Wonder how they know that and talk about the instruments they use to measure wind direction and speed. Do they talk about "wind chill?" Explain what that means. Ask the children if they have ever noticed the wind carrying or moving things. Plan to go outside on the next windy day to see. Check the "After the Walk" section for directions on how to make weather vanes, pinwheels, wind skippers and other things to help you in your wind exploration. After your initial walk, you may want to try several different outdoor investigations of the wind to observe and raise questions about it.

Demonstration

Make a simple weather vane and show it to the children. Blow on or fan the tail section of the vane to make it move, doing so from several different directions. Explain that the tail section will move until it no longer feels force on either side and the arrow will point directly to the source of the wind (you or the fan). Explain that this is pointing "into the wind," and is an indication of the direction from which the wind is coming. Wind direction is always reported in terms of where it is coming from. If the arrow on the weather vane points to the west, the wind is coming from the west and going to the east (the direction where the tail rests).

On the Walk / Ideas for Exploring

Observing

Look at some trees to see if you can notice signs of the wind. Are the leaves and branches moving? Do they seem to move more at the top of the tree or near the bottom? Are there some trees moving and some not moving? Notice how the movement of the trees relates to the intensity of the wind.

Notice how flowers, plants and shrubs are affected by the wind. Does the thickness of the leaves or clusters of branches make any difference? Which plants seem to be most affected by the wind? What does wind do to some of the flower petals?

Does the location of the trees or plants make any difference? Do things blow more if they are out in the open or up against a house or wall? Do they blow more on one side of the house or the other side? Wonder why that might be and if it would always be the same.

What other parts of trees or plants are blown by the wind? Do you see seeds, or fluff from any plant life being transported by the wind? Look for some things you might pick to observe how wind will affect them. Try to find dandelion fluff, silk from milkweed pods, cotton fluff from some trees and other seeds.

Notice how the wind affects other things in the environment such as clothes hanging on lines, dust or debris along the walk, water from hoses or sprinklers or in ponds, smoke from chimneys, flags, hanging planters, lights or wind chimes, awnings, and so on. Look at the clouds and see if they are moving. Talk about what makes the clouds move.

Notice the wind blowing peoples' clothing, hair, or the things they are holding or using.

Take along some streamers to let the children hold in the wind and observe. Have them hold the streamers in several different positions and directions to observe the effect of the wind. Take along a wind skipper and lay it on the ground to observe the effect of ground breezes.

Blow bubbles in the wind and see what happens.

Sensing

Listen to the sounds related to the wind. Ask the children what sounds they hear: leaves rustling, things flapping, whistling or humming sounds. Can you decide if the wind itself makes the sounds, or is it the things the wind is moving? Do the sounds get louder or softer or change in any way? What contributes to those changes?

Talk about how the wind feels blowing in your face or blowing your hair or clothes. Have the children turn in different directions to see if it feels different. Run into and away from the wind to see how that feels. Are there sudden gusts of wind that feel different? Is it colder facing the wind?

Have the children shout into the wind to see what happens to their voices. Are they as loud as usual? Can they hear each other over the wind?

Are there any other sensations the wind produces such as special aromas or gritty textures from dust?

Let the children imitate the sounds of the wind and make up short stories about the wind and how it feels.

Experimenting

Use your weather vane to decide on the direction of the wind. Does the wind's direction stay constant or does it change? Repeat this on several different days, recording the wind's direction.

Use a simple homemade anemometer to see how fast the wind is blowing. Count the number of times the spoons rotate in one minute and use that as your own measurement of wind speed. Repeat several different times to see if the speed is the same or if it changes. Take some measurements when the wind is gusting so you can talk about what that means.

Have the children try holding different items in the wind such as flags, balloons, pin wheels, different kinds of kites. See what happens. On a very windy day, hold up some white strips of textured cloth, such as terry cloth, to see if they pick up any dust from the wind. Do they catch any other things like seeds blowing in the wind?

Have the children experiment with objects of different weight to see how the wind affects them. What happens to things like balloons, feathers, papers, rocks, blocks and so on when they are left in the wind? Try tossing a homemade parachute around to see what the wind does to it. Try throwing different weight balls around, such as beach balls, sponge balls, rubber balls and different frisbees. See if the wind has any effect on where they go or land. Practice flying paper and styrofoam planes.

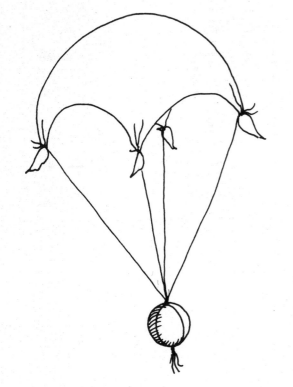

After the Walk / Follow-up Activities

Discussion

Talk about the things you observed and did on the walk. Let the children tell you the things they remember. Write up a list of some generalizations about the wind and use them for a book or chart about the wind.

Talk about how wind can be used for power and show the children some pictures of windmills. Think about how the wind blew the pinwheels and other things the children took outside. Explain that windmills have large blades on them to catch the wind. As the wind turns the blades, the force is used to run a generator connected to the windmill. Long ago wind was used in that way to turn wheels that milled or ground grain into flour, hence the name "windmill." Windmills are now used mainly to pump water or to drive electric generators for power.

Look at pictures showing the effect of wind on land and water. Talk about those effects. Include some storm pictures and some with people in them. Talk about the different types of wind storms such as hurricanes, blizzards and tornadoes. Let the children share what they may have heard about those kinds of storms. Think about keeping safe during such storms and how weather forecasting helps people plan for safety.

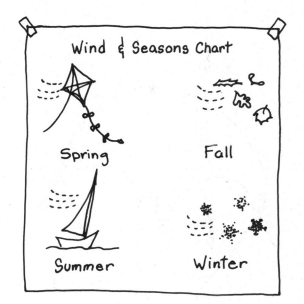

Wind and Seasons Chart

Make a chart showing the wind in different seasons. Some things to include would be trees and leaves for fall, kites for spring, sail boats for summer, and blowing snow and bare branches or pine trees for winter.

Demonstration

Talk about the relationship of the wind to the weather. Blow up a balloon and release the air in it to let the children feel the wind it makes. Explain that air always moves from a place where pressure is high (inside the balloon) to a place where it is low. The bigger the difference in the high and low pressure areas, the faster the air moves or the harder the wind blows. Blow up the balloon again and hold a little ball of cotton in front of it. This time when you release the air, let it catch the cotton ball and move it. Try this a few times, pointing the air in different directions. Discuss how the wind moves the clouds along and thus transports our weather systems.

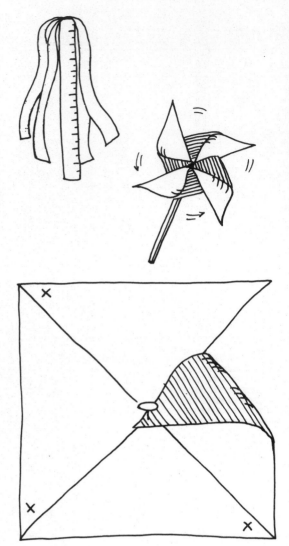

Things to Fly

Make kites, pinwheels, streamers, wind skippers, flags and airplanes to fly in the wind. Make streamers using different weights of paper, from strips of tissue paper to strips of heavy construction paper. Test how the wind affects them. Attach the strips to a dowel or stick. Also make streamers from strips of corduroy, silk and other cloths.

Make airplanes from folded paper and from styrofoam trays.

To make a <u>wind skipper</u>, cut a circle from a 10" tagboard square or use a 10" paper plate. Cut spokes from the center to 2" from the edge of the circle. Fold the wedges up and down in an alternate pattern.

Wind Instruments

Show the children pictures of wind instruments. Think about the sounds the wind makes. Explain that wind instruments are played by blowing into them. Have the children blow and make sounds like the wind. Have them try holding their mouths in different shapes to control the sound and also cup their hands around their mouths to see how that affects the sound. Make kazoos by covering one end of a toilet paper tube with wax paper secured by a rubber band. Poke a hole near the covered end. Children hum into the open end of the kazoo to see what happens. Make some with two or three holes to see if that changes the sound. Explain that the curves and number of holes on a wind instrument influence the way the sound will come out, and that the person playing the instrument can control the sound by opening and closing those holes (as the children can on their kazoos).

List all the instruments that are played by blowing. Explain that the ones made of wood are called woodwinds, while the others are called brass.

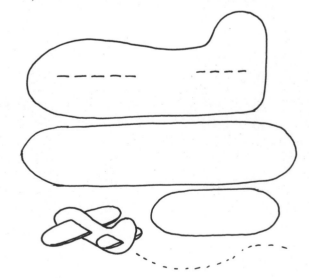

Measuring the Wind

Make some weather vanes: A very simple vane can be made using a straw attached by a straight pin to the eraser of a pencil. Move the pin up and down a few times to make the hole large enough for the straw to turn freely. Make a slit at one end of the straw and slide a tagboard arrowhead into that slit. Place a long feather into the opening of the straw at the other end, securing it with a very small amount of a gummy substance such as "hold-it" or clay or gum. If you wish to hold the vane further away than arms length, tape the pencil to a stick.

A more complex vane that includes direction indicators can be made using straws, thin tagboard, toothpicks, a knitting needle, cork and a styrofoam base. To make the vane part, seal one end of a piece of a straw with a gummy substance or sealing wax. Place a second piece of a straw in the gum or wax perpendicular to the first straw. Flatten the two ends of that straw and glue a small tagboard arrowhead to one end, and a larger tail section to the other end. Assemble the base of your vane by inserting the knitting needle through the small styrofoam base and then through the cork. Slip the straw vane onto the knitting needle. Insert the four toothpicks into the cork so they are all at right angles. To the toothpicks, attach small cards with direction indicators (N, S, E, W) written on them. The important thing in making vanes is that the tail section be much larger than the arrow.

An anemometer can be made in much the same way as the second vane. Use three or four small plastic spoons (one of a different color) inserted into the gummy material at the top of a section of drinking straw and slip over the knitting needle. Count the rotations per minute by counting the times the colored spoon passes a set mark.

Measure the wind on several days and keep a chart of your readings. Give your own weather reports using your own measures.

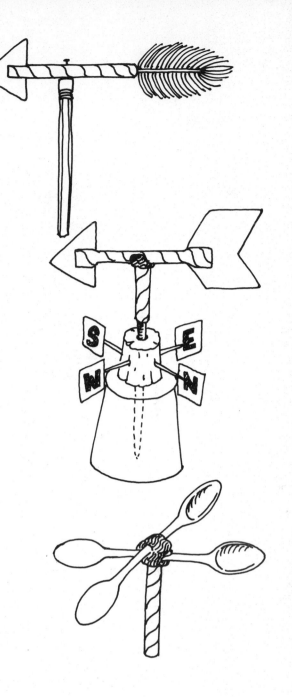

Wind Chimes

Make wind chimes to hang outside. Poke several holes in an aluminum pie tin. Knot several strings and suspend them through the holes in the pie tins. To these strings tie nails, bolts, nuts, bells, large metal paper clips and anything that will make noise when it is blown into contact with the other objects. Attach a heavier string to the center of the pie tin that can be used to hang the wind chime.

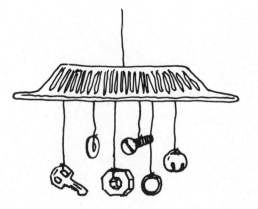

81

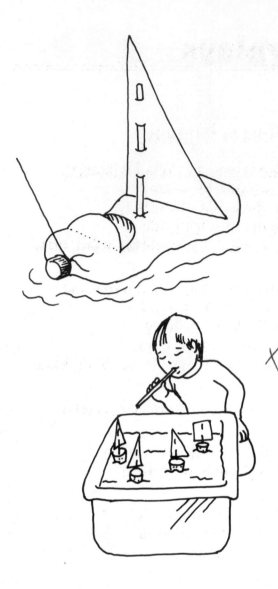

Make Sail Boats

Make sail boats from plastic dish detergent bottles. Poke a hole on one side of the bottle and cut a half-moon slit at the end of the same side and fold up. Be sure cap is in closed position and glue to bottle. Cut a triangle or rectangle from a plastic bleach bottle to form the sail. Poke some holes along the longer edge of the sail and insert a skewer or dowel through those holes. Place the dowel into the hole in the dish detergent bottle. Float sail boats in large water tub. Make some with rectangular sails and some with triangular sails to see which shape sails better. Fan them or blow on them to make them go. Use a balloon to create a bigger wind to see what that does to the sail boats. Try these outdoors in a pond as well, attaching strings so they don't blow too far away.

Sailboats can also be made from corks. Cut small paper triangles for sails. Insert a toothpick into one side of the sail and then into the cork. Use in a dish pan filled with water and have the children blow on them through straws. You may want to have a few races. Number or decorate the sails so you can keep track of them during the race.

Make Parachutes

Use a two-foot square of cloth, a ball and some string to make a parachute. Take four pieces of string of equal length and attach one piece to each corner of the cloth. Wrap the other ends of the strings around the ball so they enclose it and tie securely. Toss in the air and let your parachute float down. Do this indoors and outdoors to see what difference the wind makes in the way the parachute moves.

Large Motor or Rhythmic Activities

Run with streamers or scarves to imitate what happens outdoors in the wind.

Make pretend windmills. Children stand back to back and move their arms in opposite patterns.

Wind and Weather Mural

Make a mural showing different kinds of clouds and weather. Use cotton for the clouds. Toss some cotton balls in black powdered tempera in a paper bag to get some dark stormy clouds. Have the children draw on the mural or paste on some pictures from magazines showing different types of weather.

Songs, Poems and Fingerplays

To the tune of "Frere Jacque"

Wind is Blowing

Wind is blowing. Wind is blowing.
All around, all around.
See the leaves go twirling
See the dust it's swirling.
Blow, wind, blow—blow, wind, blow.

Let the children pretend to be twirling leaves

Wind is blowing. Wind is blowing.
All around, all around.
See the kites go flying
Run and keep on trying.
Blow, wind, blow—blow, wind, blow.

Have children pretend to run and fly kites

(Add additional seasonal verses:)

See the snow flakes twirling
Into drifts they're swirling.

See the boats go sailing
With their sails aflailing.

Oh How the Wind Does Blow

To the tune of "Over the River and Through the Woods"

Over the ground and through the trees
Oh, how the wind does blow.
It moves the leaves or clouds or snow
Everywhere it goes.

Over the ground and through the trees,
The wind keeps blowing so.
It bends the branches to and fro
And hums so very low—oh.

Over the ground and through the trees
Oh how the wind does blow.
It blows my hair and scarf around
And every other thing it's found!

The Wind

The wind is blowing very hard,
It's blowing things into my yard.
Papers, twigs and all those leaves
And many, many types of seeds.

It blows the clouds along the sky
And flaps the clothes on the lines nearby.
It makes the smoke from chimneys curl
And all the flags it does unfurl.

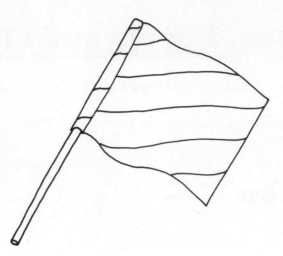

Hold up four fingers on one hand

Make flutter motion with other hand

Hold up three fingers

Make fluttering motion

Hold up two fingers

Make wind motions

Hold up one finger

Four Little Leaves

Four little leaves
On the branch of a tree.
Along came the wind,
And then there were three.

Three little leaves in the
Morning dew.
The wind fluttered by,
And then there were two.

Two little leaves
Waving in the sun.
A sudden gust of wind,
And then there was one.

One little leaf
Hanging up there,
The wind shook that branch,
And now it is bare.

Windy Day Walk

We went for a walk one windy day
And found before too long
That if we turned the other way
The wind helped us along!

Start walking in one direction

Turn around and walk in other direction

Wind Chill

As we went walking one winter day
Into the wind so strong
We turned around before too long
And walked another way!

Start walking in one direction

Have children walk backwards

84

And more

The Baby Fir Trees from **Sing A Song.** Lucille Wood and Roberta McLaughlin. Prentice-Hall, 1960.

I Am a Pine Tree from **Singing Fun.** Lucille Wood and Louise Scott. Webster, 1954.

My Kite, Washing Clothes, The Wind, from **Finger Frolics.** Liz Cromwell and Dixie Hibner. Partner, 1976.

Books

Barrett, Judi, **The Wind Thief.** Atheneum, 1977.

Black, Irma Simonton. **Busy Winds.** Holiday, 1968.

Broekel, Ray. **Storms** (A New True Book Series). Childrens Press, 1982.

Brown, Margaret Wise. **When the Wind Blew.** Harper & Row, 1977.

dePaola, Tomie. **The Cloud Book.** Scholastic, 1975.

Elliott, Alan C. **On Sunday the Wind Came.** Morrow, 1980.

Ets, Marie Hall. **Gilberto and the Wind.** Viking, 1963.

Garrison, Christian. **Little Pieces of the West Wind.** Bradbury, 1975.

Hutchins, Pat. **The Wind Blew.** MacMillan, 1974.

Keats, Ezra. **A Letter to Amy.** Harper & Row, 1968.

LaFontaine, Jean de. **The North Wind and the Sun.** Watts, 1965.

Lexau, Joan M. **Who Took The Farmers Hat?** Harper & Row, 1967.

Mizumura, Kazue. **I See the Winds.** Crowell, 1966.

O'Neill, Mary. **Winds.** Doubleday, 1970.

Schick, Eleanor. **City in the Winter.** MacMillan, 1970.

Thompson, Brenda and Cynthia Overback. **The Winds That Blow.** Lerner, 1977.

Tresselt, Alvin. **Follow the Wind.** Lothrop, 1950.

Tresselt, Alvin. **The Wind and Peter.** Oxford University, 1948.

Ungerer, Tomi. **The Hat.** Parents, 1970.

Zolatow, Charlotte. **The Storm Book.** Harper & Row, 1952.

Zolatow, Charlotte. **When the Wind Stops.** Abelard-Schuman, 1962.

THE COMMUNITY AT LARGE

Bank

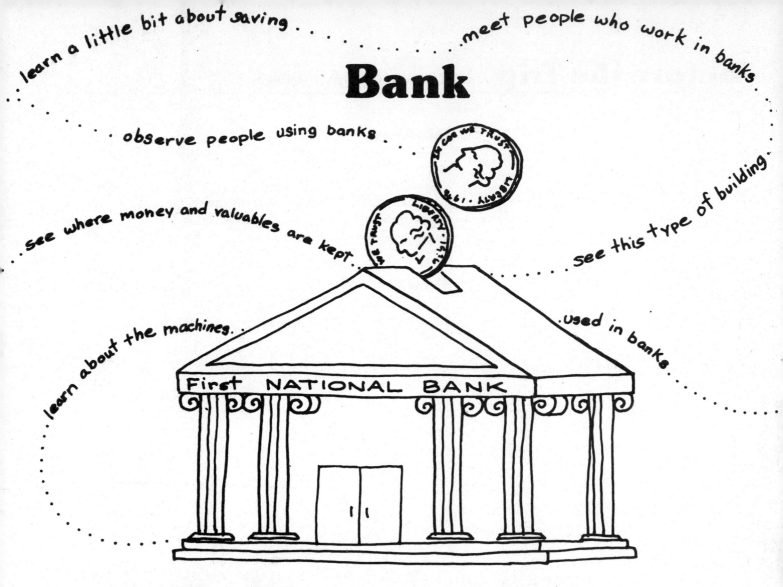

...learn a little bit about saving... ...meet people who work in banks...
...observe people using banks...
...see where money and valuables are kept... ...see this type of building...
...learn about the machines... ...used in banks...

First NATIONAL BANK

Some Words to Learn and Use

banker   clerk   secretary   teller   deposit   check

savings account   money   vault   safe   guard

computer   bank windows   bookkeeper   borrow

withdrawal slip   checkbook   penny   nickel   dime

quarter   dollar   copper   silver   safety deposit box

cash machine   passcard   loan   mortgage   security

calculator

Talk About

Ask the children what they do with any money they receive. Where do they keep it? Where do their parents keep money? Let the children suggest good places to keep money and discuss what attributes places for safe-keeping should have. Ask the children why people need money. What would we do if there were no money?

Show and Tell

Show the children your own checkbook. Explain how checks work and that people use checks instead of money sometimes.

On the Trip / Ideas for Exploring

Observing

Notice the appearance of the bank on the outside as well as inside. Is it old or new? What types of materials are used in its construction and furnishings? Are there pictures on the walls? Look at the people who work at the bank and notice if they are wearing any special clothes.

Look at any signs around the bank and tell the children what they say.

Notice the way the bank is organized with desk areas, offices, tellers' windows and closed-in spaces. Point out any machines you can readily see, such as typewriters, coin machines, computers, money machine, and copiers.

Observe people transacting business in the bank.

Be sure to visit the vault area and notice the huge doors and any automatic locking system on the vault. Peek inside to see all the safety deposit boxes. Talk about what people would keep in safety deposit boxes, and why those things would be kept there.

Observe the auto-bank or drive-up window area and watch how that operation works.

Asking

Ask a person (or several people) to tell you about the work they do at the bank. Learn as much as you can in the simplest terms possible about the different jobs in the bank such as teller, receptionist, loan officer, president, and vice president.

Ask to see the safe and the back office area. Show the children the packages of coins and how the money is organized, sorted and stored.

Let the children ask questions, too. They are bound to ask very interesting ones.

Ask people to show the children how various machines in the bank work. Children will even be fascinated by a photocopying machine, let alone calculators and money machines.

Speculating

Wonder what the people talking to the bank personnel at various desks are doing. Are they opening new accounts or negotiating loans? Ask the children what people use loans for. Try to guess what these customers are planning to do with any loans.

Guess where the president and vice presidents of the bank work. How can they tell?

Talking About

Discuss the atmosphere in the bank and think about why it looks the way it does. Is it noisy, quiet, attractive? Would it be a good place to work?

Think about the way the bank works. Think about how people put money in the bank and then use it. How does the bank keep track of it? How do people know how much money they have in the bank when they keep using it?

Talk about the way security boxes are protected. How do people get into that area? How are the locked boxes opened?

Collecting

Bring back samples of deposit slips, checks, withdrawal slips, bank books, loan applications, bank statements and anything else they'll give you to use to play "bank."

After the Trip / Follow-up Activities

Discussion

Talk about the trip. Let the children share their experiences.

Talk about saving money and keeping it safe so it doesn't get lost. Discuss savings accounts and checking accounts.

Show and discuss checkbooks, bank books, deposit and withdrawal slips. How is writing a check similar to writing a letter? Explain the deposit slips and how they are used. Make small deposit books and checkbooks to use in bank play.

Piggy Banks

Make piggy banks out of baby food jars, cocoa or other small cans. Have children decorate them.

Our Big Book About Banks

Make a group book about the things you saw in the bank. Look for pictures from newspapers or magazines of things seen at the bank and put them in your book. Write the names by the items and talk about their uses.

How Much Is It?

Make How Much Is It? cards to use with the group to help children discover which coin is worth more. You will need four pieces of cardboard 6$\frac{1}{2}$" by 7" and four pieces 3$\frac{1}{2}$" by 6$\frac{1}{2}$". Tape a larger and smaller card together so that the smaller one can fold over the larger one and cover up the lower half of it. On the top of each larger card glue or tape one real coin (penny, nickel, dime, quarter). Write the name of the coin below the coin and then the number of pennies in that coin. On the bottom half of the card glue or tape the correct number of pennies. When the smaller card is folded up the real pennies and the numeral telling the correct amount should be covered up so the children can guess how many it's going to be.

Games

With older children, play a simplified version of Monopoly. For younger children play Put-and-Take type games using play money or poker chips. Some chips or coins are given to each child and some are placed in center of players. A spinner dial or stack of cards can be made that tells each child how many to take from or add to the center.

Coin Display

Display various kinds of coins and bills. Note size, shape and pictures. Display samples of coins from other countries. Talk about coins and their differences.

Play Money Matching Game

Make a play money matching game. Make a master board with a penny, nickel, dime and quarter on one side of the board and on the other side draw circles for amounts to correspond with each coin. Make play money coins to use in the matching game by having the children lay paper over real coins and do rubbings. Cut out and laminate. If you wish, the coins can be mounted on copper or silver colored paper to look more realistic. You will need 41 pennies, nine nickels, four dimes and one quarter. Children match the play coins using the circles drawn on the master board as a guide for the correct combinations equalling each coin.

Variation: Make a similar set out of felt to use on the felt board.

Dramatic Play

Set up a play money, checkers or buttons bank. Children deposit "money." They can then write checks for friends to cash, or they can make a withdrawal themselves. Children take turns being tellers and customers.

Add an old check writing machine (if you can find one), stamp pad, cash register and other props to your "play bank."

Make a vault out of a large, heavy cardboard box or crate. Use a combination lock on it. Store extra "money" in it. For bank play, tellers come to get extra play money, checkers or buttons from the vault for the day's business.

If you wish, add a drive-up window area to your bank. Use small cans with plastic covers as your tubes to pass from car to window. Or envelopes can be placed on a dust pan extended from the clerk at the window. Children can use wheel toys to drive up to the window!

Songs, Poems and Fingerplays

Four Bright Coins

Four bright coins shining at me,
The first one said "I'm a penny you see."
The second one said "How do you do?"
"I'm called a nickel and I'm bigger than you!"
The third one said "You're both small stuff,"
"If you want to buy something, you're not enough."
"But look at me, I'm small and I shine,"
"But I can buy something 'cuz I'm a dime."
The last coin looked at them all and laughed,
"All of you together don't measure up to me,"
"'Cuz I'm a quarter, can't you see!"

Tape coins to large Popsicle sticks and have children hold up the appropriate coin for each part of the verse

The Auto Bank

Pretend to drive car

Pretend to fill a container

Swoop arm down and back
Pretend to open container

My Mommy drove to the bank today,
To the drive-up window without delay,
Put checks in a tube which whooshed away.
Soon the whoosh was heard once more,
And the tube was back with money for the store.
And then guess what I heard it say?
"Thank you," and "Have a nice day."

In the Bank

In the bank, in the bank,
There's a safe, there's a safe.
Safe to keep our money, safe to keep our money,
Safe, safe, safe. Safe, safe, safe.

This is the Way

This is the way we save our money,
Save our money, save our money.
This is the way we save our money,
We put it in the bank.

Pretend to drop coins in bank

This is the way we write a check,
Write a check, write a check.
This is the way we write a check
When we go to the bank.

Pretend to write

This is the way we spend our money,
Spend our money, spend our money.
This is the way we spend our money,
When we go to the store.

Pretend to pay for something

Chant

One-a-Penny

One-a-penny, two-a-penny, three-a-penny, four,
Four-a-penny, five-a-penny, that's a nickel more.

Six-a-penny, seven-a-penny, eight-a-penny, more,
Nine-a-penny, ten-a-penny, that's a dime for the store.

And more

I've Got Sixpence, Jolly Jolly Sixpence (English folk song)

Five Brown Pennies, from **Rhymes for Fingers and Flannelboards.** Louise Binder Scott and
    J. J. Thompson. McGraw-Hill, 1960.

Books

Baker, Eugene. **I Want to Be a Bank Teller.** Childrens Press, 1972.

Bellak, Rhoda and Dick Voehl. **Five Pennies Make a Nickel—A Child's First Savings
    Book.** Wanderer, 1981.

Brown, Kristin. **Fun With Money.** Western, 1982.

Davis, Mary. **Careers in a Bank.** Lerner, 1973.

Elkin, Benjamin. **The True Book of Money.** Childrens Press, 1960.

German, Donald R. **Money and Banks.** Dandelion, 1979.

German, Joan. **The Money Book.** Lodestar, 1981.

Gross, Ruth. **Money, Money, Money.** Scholastic, 1976.

James, Elizabeth and Carol Barkin. **What Is Money?** Raintree, 1977.

Maher, John E. **Ideas About Money.** Watts, 1970.

Oppenheim, Joanne. **Cents Sense.** Milton Bradley, 1983.

Pope, Billy. **Let's Visit a Bank.** Taylor, 1975.

Rosenberg, Amyl. **My Cash Register Book.** Simon & Schuster, 1981.

Schwartz, Alvin. **Stores.** MacMillan, 1977.

Sootin, Laura. **Let's Go to the Bank.** Putnam, 1957.

Ziegler, Sandra. **Something for Sara: A Beginning Book About Money.** Child's World,
    1977.

Car Dealership

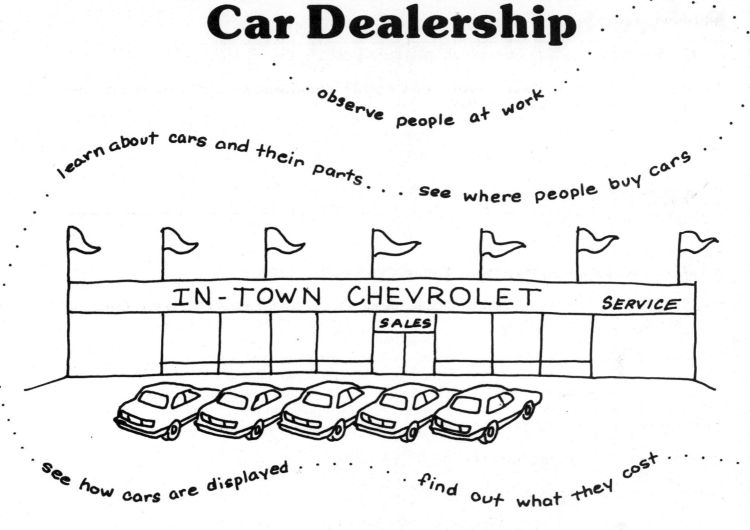

observe people at work

learn about cars and their parts. . . . see where people buy cars

IN-TOWN CHEVROLET   SERVICE

SALES

see how cars are displayed . . . . find out what they cost

Some Words to Learn and Use

model   sports car   station wagon   compact   sedan

two-door   four-door   convertible   hardtop   hatchback

new   used car lot   showroom   sticker price   hood

hub cap   trunk   fender   wheels   tires   rubber

whitewalls   radials   car radio   steering wheel   brakes

stick shift   automatic   upholstery   windshield wiper

tinted glass   seat belts   bucket seats   armrest

dashboard   horn   speedometer   tachometer

headlights   bumper   grill   hood ornament

Before the Trip / Introductory Activities

Talk About

Ask the children if their families have cars. If so, do they know what kinds they are? Did they get their cars from a private person or a car dealer? Have they ever been to see where people can buy cars?

Talk about cars that are made in this country. Name some of them. Then talk about cars made in other countries and name some of them; explain that we call those cars "foreign" (meaning from other countries).

Show and Tell

Bring in some toy cars of many different types. Ask the children to bring in some of theirs. Talk about all the different models. Are those models still around or are they "antiques" from a long time ago? Ask if they would like to visit a place where people can buy cars now. Get a catalog from a dealership you plan to visit. Can the children tell what make of car is in the catalog? Find out how they know or recognize that make.

On the Trip / Ideas for Exploring

Observing

Notice the appearance of the building and any lots near it. Are there flags, balloons, or other decorations around? Are there big glass windows all around the building? Wonder why they have such big windows. Is there writing on the windows?

Look at the cars that are outside in the lot and see if you can tell whether they are new or used. Are there other vehicles besides cars for sale? Is there writing on the cars too? Look for any signs or information about the cars. Are they all the same make? How can you recognize different makes?

Notice all the different sections of the building. Is there a special area for looking at the cars (showroom) and other work areas like a service department or body shop? Notice all the different entrances into the building area. Are there entrances for cars as well as people?

Notice the cars or any other vehicles on display inside the building. Are they displayed in a special way? How can you find out what features those cars have? Are there sales tickets on them?

Point out and name specific parts of the cars on display: hood, gas tank, bumper, fender and so forth. Note the ones that vary. There may be a trunk on some models, hatchback on others.

Look for special identifying features of cars and note especially the grillwork, hood ornaments and names written on the car's body.

Notice the different clothes worn by the people working in different parts of the dealership. Are there special outfits for salespeople, service managers, and mechanics that identify them as working for this particular agency?

Ask a salesperson to tell you something about the cars on display. How much do they cost? Have him point out the additional cost of things called "special features." Look at some examples of special features (electric windows, air conditioning, spokes in the hub caps).

How do people arrange to pay for cars? Does the dealer take cars in trade?

Can the salesperson tell you what features are most popular with the public? What models are the biggest sellers? Is any color especially popular?

Ask if the children can sit in the cars and let them take turns trying out the front and back seats of the cars. Be sure to point out and name the inside parts of the car: steering wheel, brake, clutch, accelerator, glove compartment, dashboard, seat belts, and so forth.

Ask about the work different people do in the car dealership. What system do they use to keep track of the cars they have available and the customers whose cars are under guarantee? Ask to see the different work areas and any special machines or equipment used in those areas.

Comparing

Count the wheels, doors, windows, lights, seats and other parts of cars. Are all of these the same on all models?

Compare color, paint finishes, and decorative trim on different models. Which colors and/or styles do the children like best?

Compare sizes of different models. Compare sizes of specific parts such as tires and trunks. Look at how seating capacity changes with the size of the car. To aid in your comparison, measure some parts or ask the salesperson for dimensions of different models.

What other comparisons can you make that are less visible, such as engine horsepower and miles per gallon?

Look at pictures of other cars in catalogs the dealership may have. Compare those to the models you see on display.

Speculating

Wonder why people decide to buy new cars. Ask the children to give you their ideas. Wonder why people pick certain cars and not others.

Think about why the car dealership is decorated with all those balloons, flags, and bright colors.

Wonder where the word "horse power" came from and what it means.

After the Trip / Follow-up Activities

Discussion

Ask the children again about their own families' cars. See if they can tell you more about them.

Make up a story about which kinds of cars the children would like when they grow up. Use pictures cut from lots of catalogs to help illustrate the story. Write a description taken from each child's idea about what kind of car the child would like. Have the child find a picture to accompany it. Put the pictures and descriptions together into some kind of book or scroll.

Number or Color Matching Game: Cars and Garages

Make garages by cutting the top off a milk carton. Cover with paper and write a number from one to five (10 for older children) on each garage. Assemble a set of five plastic cars that will fit into the milk cartons. Using gummed paper or coding dots, mark the cars with dots or numbers to match the numerals on each garage.

- To match numerals, simply paste a number on each car and have the children drive the car to the matching garage.
- To teach the concept that each number represents specific quantity, mark each car with coding dots ranging from one to five. Children now match the number of dots on a car to the corresponding numeral on a garage.
- For a color identification game, use different colored cars and cover the garages with paper in the same colors.

Dramatic Play Area

Set up a table-top dramatic play area to resemble a dealership showroom. Decorate with bright-colored flags or banners made by the children. Have model cars on display and lots of catalogs to look at. Write up signs for specials and signs to tell about features of the cars on display. During free play times, children can pretend to order cars or take them out on loan.

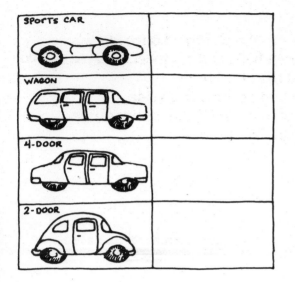

Large Motor Activity

Let the children sit on the floor with legs extended, pretending to be cars driving along the road. Have them move forward or backward by moving their buttocks and legs (an excellent exercise). Give directions to have them go fast, go slow, stop for stop lights, and so forth. Have them pretend to steer, shift gears, or use turn signals as you direct.

Matching Games

Make matching games and/or lotto games using car seals or wrapping paper with car pictures. Catalogs from car dealers or from sets of match-box cars can also be used to make games. For simple matching or lotto games, children find the cars that are the same.

Also make a model matching game. Cut out pictures of different models, such as stationwagon, sports cars, two-door, four-door, and compact. On a master board, paste one picture at the start of each row. Paste other pictures on cards. Children find the pictures that are the same model or type to match the first car in each row.

Car Showroom Mural

Make a mural of a car dealership. Show the large lots of cars, the building and all the decorations. Use cut out pictures of cars or let the children draw their own. Cutout paper shapes can be pasted for flags and balloons.

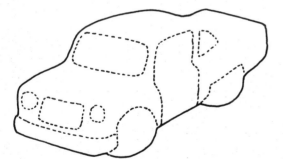

Cut - Paper Cars

Cut out shapes of paper and let the children put them together to make cars. You will need small circles, larger-sized half circles, rectangles that are curved on one side, and some different sized rectangles.

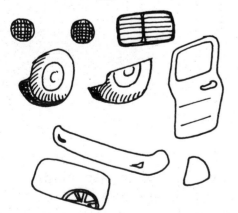

Diagram of Car

Draw a large diagram of a car, indicating its various parts. Cut out pictures of car parts from car catalogs. Let the children match the parts (hood, tires, roof, trunk, windshield, windshield wiper) to the larger diagram. Mount on bulletin board and use push pins to attach parts to the appropriate spots.

Songs, Poems and Fingerplays

To the tune of "Three Little Ducks That I Once Knew"; or use as a chant

Hold up three fingers
Hold up two fingers
Hold up one finger

Put palms together and move hands forward in quick weaving motion

Five New Cars

Five new cars on the showroom floor.
Someone bought the compact
And now there are four.

Four new cars that we can see.
Away goes the wagon
And now there are three.

Three new cars the salesman shows to you.
Off goes the sports car
And now there are two.

Two new cars: see a mother and her son.
They took the blue one
And now there is one.

One new car just as plain as can be.
But it's just right for
My family and me.

So we bought the last one
From the showroom floor.
And now we can't see anymore.

To the tune of "Mexican Hat Song"

Three Little Cars

Three little cars that I once knew,
Hatch-back and compact, that made two.
But the one little car
With the stripes on its side,
It ruled the road with its overdrive.
Zoom, zoom, zoom.

Hold up appropriate number of fingers

Can also be used with pictures of cars on a flannel board. Children remove the pictures as described

My Car

My car it has four tires (clap, clap)
Four tires has my car (clap, clap)
And had it not four tires (clap, clap)
My car couldn't go very far! (clap, clap)

The Wheels on the Car

To the tune of "The Wheels on the Bus"

The wheels on the car go round and round,
Round and round, round and round.
The wheels on the car go round and round,
All through the town.

The doors on the car go open and shut.
The wipers on the car go swish, swish, swish.

The lights on the car go blink, blink, blink.
The horn on the car goes beep, beep, beep.   (Make up additional verses)

And more

Click-Clack, from **Finger Frolics.** Liz Cromwell and Dixie Hibner. Partner, 1976.

Books

Alexander, Anne. **ABC of Cars and Trucks.** Doubleday, 1956.

Benson, Christopher. **Careers in Auto Sales and Service.** Lerner, 1974.

Burningham, John. **Mr. Gumpy's Motor Car.** Harper & Row, 1976.

Carrie, Christopher. **Amazing Cars.** Binney & Smith, 1981.

Cummings, W. T. **Miss Esta Maude's Secret.** McGraw-Hill, 1961.

Ets, Marie Hall. **Little Old Automobile.** Viking, 1948.

Fisher, Barbara. **Car Boy.** Ten Penny, 1977.

Hall, Adelaide. **ABC of Cars, Trucks and Machines.** McGraw-Hill, 1970.

Lenski, Lois. **The Little Auto.** McKay, 1942.

Radlauer, Edward. **Model Cars.** Childrens Press, 1977.

Wilkinson, Sylvia. **Automobiles.** Childrens Press, 1982.

Wooley, Catherine. **Charley and the New Car.** Morrow, 1957.

Young, Miriam Burt. **If I Drove A Car.** Lothrop, 1971.

For teacher reference and use:

Spier, Peter. **Tin Lizzie.** Doubleday, 1975.

Construction Site

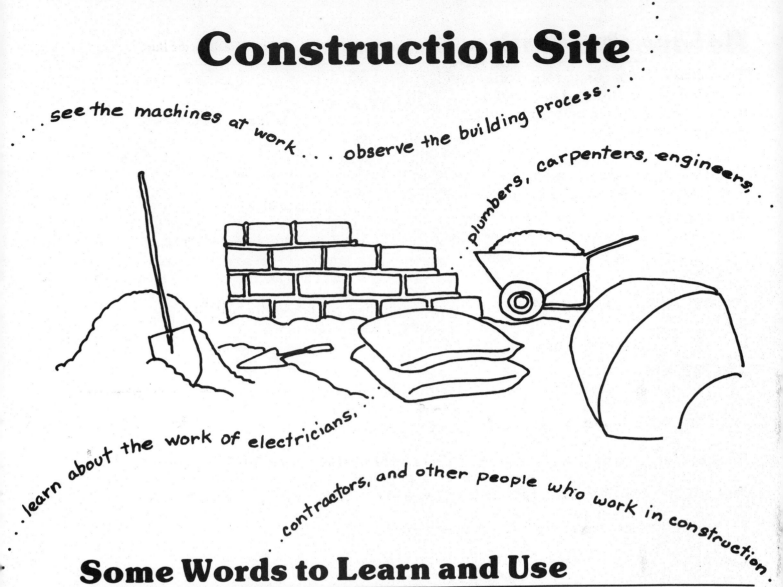

...see the machines at work . . . observe the building process . . . plumbers, carpenters, engineers, . . . learn about the work of electricians, . . . contractors, and other people who work in construction

Some Words to Learn and Use

digging   excavate   contractor   electrician   steamfitter

ducts   wiring   plumber   pipes   blueprints   carpenter

cement   concrete blocks   foundation   bricks

bricklayer   framing   roof beam   rafters   hard hats

sheetrock   girders   tractor   bulldozer   dump truck

power shovel   back hoe   crane   wall   skyscraper

grade   scraper   prefabricated   insulation

Before the Walk / Introductory Activities

Read and Talk About

Read the story **Mike Mulligan and His Steam Shovel.** Talk about the kind of excavators used in construction now and think about how they avoid the problem Mike Mulligan faced. Plan to visit a construction site and ask.

Ask the children if they have noticed any buildings being built. What did they see at the construction site? List some questions the children raise and plan to talk to someone in construction to get some answers. Arrange to have the children visit and ask the questions themselves.

NOTE: If possible, choose a site within walking distance so that you can visit in small groups frequently throughout the construction.

On the Walk / Ideas for Exploring

Observing

Notice the collection of machinery and materials assembled at the site. Are they arranged in any particular way? Who seems to be telling people where to put things and what to do?

Watch any machines being used such as bulldozers, power shovels, dump trucks, cement mixers. Stay well out of the way of machines in use, but find a spot where you can see them work. Talk about how they are moving and being operated. When machines are parked and not in use, it may be possible to observe them more closely to see how they work. Notice, for instance, that many machines are made up of special parts like a bulldozer blade or a crane attached to a tractor.

Try to observe various phases of construction, such as a foundation being built, building being framed, roof beams and rafters being raised, yard being graded and finished, wiring being connected, pipes being laid and so on.

Notice any special ways the work site is prepared. Are there temporary structures on the grounds for the workmen to use? Is the area fenced off in any way?

Observe the mounting pile of debris and trash accumulating as work progresses. Is it hauled away or just added to each day? If there are useful pieces of lumber tossed on that pile, ask about taking some for the children to use.

Observe the work various people do. Notice how the people work as a team to get tasks done. Do they give directions to each other?

Do the workers wear any special clothes while at work? Do they use anything to protect their heads or eyes?

Notice any hand or power tools in use in addition to the larger machines. If power tools are in use, where does the power come from?

Asking

Ask someone to show you some of the specific machines and tell you about them. Be sure to consult with the general contractor about suitable times to ask questions. There are times when people are waiting for something or taking a break and can answer questions without interrupting their work.

If appropriate, ask how they avoid having a power shovel get stuck in the bottom of the hole it digs for the foundation.

107

If someone is mixing cement, ask how they make it. Observe how it comes out of the mixer and is transported. Ask how long it takes to harden and how quickly they have to work. Are there different types or consistencies used or is it all the same?

Tell the children as many of the names of machines and materials as you can. Ask someone to tell you the names of those items you don't know. Ask someone to show you the plans for the building. Do people keep consulting those plans?

Speculating

Can you tell what kind of building is being built? Try to guess what it might be, based on location and what you have observed so far. Does it look like any other building you've seen? Fast food restaurants tend to look alike as they go up, but they often put up signs way in advance, so there's not much left to imagine. Let the children guess anyway, as it is fun to make up ideas for the building and its use.

Wonder how much it is costing to build the building. Perhaps you can get some estimates from the builders.

Think about what would look nice around the building when it is finished.

Counting

Count the number of people working, the number of trucks or machines you see, the stacks of materials, bags of cement and other readily visible items.

You might also keep track of the number of trips the dump truck makes, or the number of times the cement mixer is loaded.

Time how long each batch of cement is mixed or how long other specific tasks take.

After the Walk / Follow-up Activities

Discussion

Talk about all the things you saw on the walk. Comment on what things are added each time you visit a site. Keep a record of how the building is progressing. Add to your running account after each visit. Keep this in a diary or log form so you can review it from time to time.

Collect pictures of buildings being built and a variety of construction sites and stages. Show the children the pictures and talk about what is going on in them.

Dramatic Play in Sand Box

Set up a construction site in your sand box. Fence off a part of the sand box to use for construction. Excavate in that area, using a steamshovel truck or plain shovels. To make a homemade scoop, mount a soup ladle onto a pulley with some strings tied both at the ladle and the handle. Raise and lower the ladle by the strings on the pulley. Turn the ladle by the handle to scoop up sand. Most likely this will be harder to use than plain shovels, but will show how complex it is to design and use machines. If you do not have a pulley, a simple one can be made with hanger wire and spools. Insert wire through the hole in the spool and bend the wire to make a bracket holding the spool. Fill dump trucks with the sand and haul to the other side of the sand box. Collect stones and rocks to use for your foundation. Mix some plaster, or use clay to cement some rocks as needed, and to insert paint stir sticks to use for framing your building. Attach pieces of cardboard to the sticks for walls. Collect a variety of toy trucks used in construction to use in your dramatic play area. Demonstrate how they work and talk about their uses. Put signs up around the construction area and let the children plan what they want to build and how long they want to pursue this activity.

Table Building Activities

Use Lego sets, Lincoln Logs, Tinker Toys, and other building material sets to construct houses or other buildings.

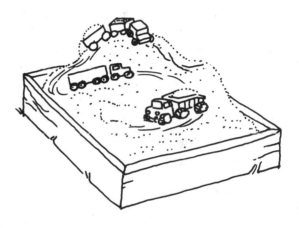

People in Construction Scroll

Talk about all the jobs that are part of construction and design a scroll that tells about the work each person does. Use builders' supply catalogs for pictures to use in your scroll. Some occupations to include in your scroll are: architects and engineers who design buildings and materials, carpenters who do all the work with lumber, bricklayers and masons who work with those materials, plumbers who put in the sewer pipes and all the plumbing, electricians who do the wiring, steamfitters and sheet metal workers who put in the heating or cooling systems and all the duct work, painters who finish the wood, and so forth. Mount the scroll on paper towel rollers. If you wish, your scroll can be used for a pretend TV series called "Building Our City." Cut up a box for a pretend TV set.

Dramatize Building

Play the record *We're Building a City* (Young People's Records), and have the children act it out. If you do not have the record, use one of the fingerplays or songs with this trip and act out all the parts.

Foundations You Can Eat

The bricks-and-mortar concept can be illustrated with a variety of food combinations that would offer fun in the making and eating. The solid substance is held together by the sticky substance and used to construct a foundation or a whole house. After the building process, the group of builders can dismantle it and eat it if they wish. Some materials to use are:

Bricks		Mortar
jello squares	and	cream cheese or whipped cream
crackers	and	peanut butter
graham crackers	and	applesauce
pieces of toast	and	soft cheddar cheese
pieces of banana, apple, or marshmallows	and	peanut butter

Invite Visitors

Invite any parents or friends who work in construction to visit your group. Ask them to bring along the tools they carry with them or a specially equipped truck the children could see. Have them tell the children about their work.

Roller Painting

Bring out some paint rollers and brushes and water and let the children pretend to paint with them, indoors on the blackboard or outdoors on any suitable wall or sidewalk.

A Book About Construction

Make up a book about different types of construction. Include pages on highways, bridges, skyscrapers, shopping malls, tunnels, airports and as many other settings as you wish. Think about the problems each kind of building presents and what would be needed for each site. Look for pictures to use in your book. Write the children's comments about how to solve design and construction problems.

Songs, Poems and Fingerplays

To the tune of "Mulberry Bush"

This is the Way We Build a House

This is the way we dig the basement
Dig the basement, dig the basement.
This is the way we dig the basement
When we build a house.

Use arms to imitate digging

Pretend to stack concrete blocks and smooth cement around them

This is the way we make the basement . . .

Pretend to hammer boards in place

This is the way we make the walls . . .

Pretend to lift very heavy beam

This is the way we hoist the roof beam . . .

(Add other verses that lend themselves to action such as: "put on the shingles," "paint the house," "lay the carpet")

The Skyscraper

Build a floor, and add a floor
And another floor I see.
Do you know how many?
I bet it's fifty-three.

Build levels, starting low and go up, up, up

Hold up five fingers on one hand and three on another

Have you ever seen a building
That went up so high?
They call it a skyscraper
Can you tell me why?

Look way up

Point to the sky

    or

'Cuz it seems to touch the sky.

The Cement Mixer

Twirl hands

Pretend to push heavy wheelbarrow
Pretend to build a brick wall

See the mixer turning round and round,
Mixing up cement pound after pound.
Fill the wheelbarrow, hurry to the site.
Smooth on the bricks, to hold them right.

111

Down at the Corner

To the tune of "Down by the Station"

Down at the corner, early in the morning,
See all the workmen gathering their things.
See all the trucks, moving to and fro.
What are they building? Do you Know?

Put fingers together to form a roof at about shoulder level

Move hands to about eye level, then above head level

Repeat motions on each level

The Houses

A one-story house, and
A two-story house, and
And a three-story house I see.
Shall we count them?
Are you ready?
One - Two - Three.

Who Builds Our House

To the tune of "The Muffin Man"

Oh, do you know an architect, an architect,
An architect, an architect?
Oh, do you know an architect,
To draw the plans for our house?

Oh, do you know a carpenter . . .
To build the frame for our house?

Oh, do you know an electrician . . .
To bring light and power to our house?

Oh, do you know a plumber . . .
To bring water and heat to our house?

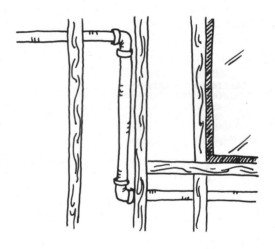

And more

The Steam Shovel, from **Let's Do Fingerplays.** M. Grayson. David McKay, 1962.

The Carpenter, from **Finger Frolics.** Liz Cromwell and Dixie Hibner. Partner, 1976.

Books

Ahlberg, Allan. **Miss Brick the Builder's Baby.** Western, 1982.

Barton, Byron. **Building a House.** Greenwillow, 1981.

Bate, Norman. **Who Built the Bridge?** Scribner, 1954.

Greenvale School, 9th Grade English Class. **Bulldozers, Loaders and Spreaders.** Doubleday, 1974.

Hoban, Tana. **Dig, Drill, Dump, Fill.** Greenwillow, 1975.

Leavitt, J. **The True Book of Tools for Building.** Childrens Press, 1961.

Mitgutsch, Ali. **From Clay to Bricks.** Carolrhoda, 1981.

Neigoff, Ann. **New House, New Town.** Whitman, 1973.

Pienkowski, Jan. **Homes.** Harvey House, 1982.

Ramos, Gloria. **Careers in Construction.** Lerner, 1975.

Rockwell, Anne and Harlan. **Machines.** MacMillan, 1972.

Scary, Richard. **What Do People Do All Day?** Random House, 1968.

Sobol, Harriet Lansam. **Pete's House.** MacMillan, 1978.

Wolde, Gunilla. **Tommy Builds a House.** Houghton-Mifflin, 1971.

Zaffo, George. **The Big Book of Real Building and Wrecking Machines.** Grosset & Dunlap, 1951.

For teacher reference and use:

Adkins, Jan. **Heavy Equipment.** Scribner, 1980.

Kelly, James E. and William Park. **The Road Builders.** Addison-Wesley, 1973.

Grocery Store

see how things are organized in a large store . . . . buy some apples . . .

OPEN DAILY 8-10 Don's Country Supermarket GROCERY PICK-UP ⬇

OUT IN

Thanks-giving Turkeys .39/#

Apples 10/1.29

Napkins .29 /w coupon

Potato Chips 99¢

Bread 3/1.39

Coffee 3# 5.99

lettuce .39

carrots 4/1.00

observe what people do who work there . . . . . learn how grocery stores work

see the variety of foods sold .

Some Words to Learn and Use

vegetables   fruits   meat   produce   bakery   section

department   delicatessen   dairy products   racks

counters   shelves   paper products   cereal

canned goods   freezer   frozen foods   condiments

spices   check-out   manager   stock clerk   carry out

conveyer belt   butcher   aisle   soft drinks   returnable

cash register   cashier   cart   bulk   generic   brand

gourmet food   coupon

Show and Taste

Bring in some fresh fruits such as oranges, grapefruit, apples, pears, bananas. Talk about them by their specific names as well as by the category of fruit (citrus) to which they belong. Examine them thoroughly and cut them open to notice their texture, seed structure, skin, and meat. Taste them. Compare and contrast their appearance, composition and taste. Ask the children if there are other kinds of fruits besides the ones you brought in, or other varieties of the same ones you sampled. Plan to go to a grocery store or super market to find out.

Talk About

Ask the children if they go shopping in grocery stores with their families. Do they know which store they've been in? What can they tell you about the stores they've been in? What have they noticed that they recall? Write down the things they tell you about the store. Plan to see if the store you visit is similar or different from the ones they describe.

On the Trip / Ideas for Exploring

Observing

Notice the general appearance of the building. Is it small, large, new, old, very busy looking or quiet? Are there any features around the building that you notice that are part of the store's operation such as an area for deliveries, a grocery pick-up area, areas for grocery carts? Is there any advertising on the windows or around the store? Observe products being delivered to the store. How are they unloaded and moved into the store?

Notice the entry way to the store. Are there double doors, automatic doors or separate entrances and exits? Is there a bulletin board with notices or other items on display to catch people's attention?

Look at the store arrangement and notice the different sections. How much can you see from the entrance area? Talk about the way things are grouped and read any large signs that tell what is in each area: meat department, produce, bakery and so forth.

Observe the check-out procedures. Are there several counters or just one? Are there special counters for just a few items or for bagging your own groceries? How do people know to which check-out to go? Notice the equipment in use. Are there conveyor belts, computerized cash registers or any other special features? Watch the cashier and the people bagging the groceries. Do they follow any system in doing their jobs? Do people carry out their own groceries, or is there a pick-up arrangement? What system do they use to keep track of people's groceries? Are there places to return bottles or other returnable containers?

Explore a few sections of the store such as the produce department and the meat department, pointing out and naming as many items as you can. Notice how things are displayed with the same type of items being grouped together. How are the display racks and counters especially suited to the items they contain? Look at the many different types of the same things: different types of apples, lettuces, ground meat and steaks.

Notice how items are packaged and marked. Call attention to how things are sold and priced. Is it by the item or by the pound? How can people decide what is a good buy? Look for signs that give price information and tell the children what different things cost.

Notice the jobs people do at the store. Do people have special tasks? Do you see people marking items for sale or replenishing shelves or packaging foods?

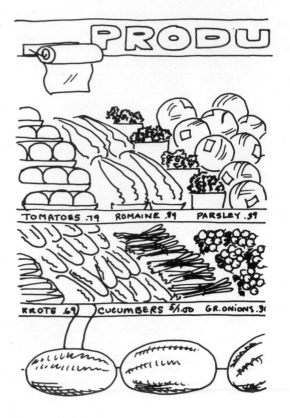

Counting and Comparing

Count the number of aisles, check-out counters, wheels on the carts, people working in each area.

Count the number of different types of the same thing such as different kinds of grapefruits, carrots, packages of bacon, brands of paper napkins, and types of pizza.

Count the different-sized containers of milk and other dairy products. Talk about the amounts in each container such as pint, quart, half gallon, gallon.

Compare the different sizes and types of some produce items such as oranges, grapefruit, tomatoes, potatoes, carrots. Be sure to note when something is a different item even though it may resemble something else. For instance, cabbage may look like lettuce, but it is actually a different vegetable.

Asking

Many large stores have special tours available for children. Call in advance to see if one can be arranged.

Ask the department managers to show you the back room work areas where items are received, wrapped or sorted. Ask them to tell you about their work.

Ask to see any special equipment they use in the store for packaging or marking. Have them demonstrate it for the children.

Ask to see the bakery kitchen or receiving area, if there is one. Notice the huge pans and storage racks for holding baked goods. If they do baking on the premises, look at the huge mixers, pans and ovens. If there is a cake decorator at work, ask for a demonstration!

Ask the butcher to show you the meat storage cooler. Ask for a demonstration or a description of how meat is trimmed and wrapped.

Speculating

Wonder why there are so many different brands of items.

Think about why so many areas of the store have things kept cold. How is that done? Why is it done? Wonder what happens in stores that don't have items kept cold. How do people shop in places without refrigeration?

What happens to the baked goods that don't get sold each day? Think about the differences of baked goods in boxes and fresh baked goods. Why can one be kept while the others have to be sold each day? Discuss the idea of preservatives.

What would it be like to work in a grocery store?

Collecting

Ask the store to give you any pictures of foods, old displays, or any other potential throwaways you might find useful.

Ask them to save plastic lids from milk containers for you. Explain that these can be used for games with children.

Buy a number of items to use in follow-up activities: apples (several different kinds); citrus fruits (one of each kind); assorted fresh vegetables (for tasting or to make soup); assorted fruits that may not be familiar to the children (pineapple or some melons); dried fruits.

After the Trip / Follow-up Activities

Discussion

Talk about the trip and ask the children what they remember about the store. How does the store you visited compare to ones they have been to before.

Ask the children if they still have questions about stores. Generate a list of things they are still curious about related to grocery stores or things they saw in the store. Plan to find some answers for them. If appropriate, plan another trip to the store to find the answers.

Play guessing games. Give clues describing a particular food and see if the children can guess what it is.

Fruit in Many Forms

Show some examples of dried fruits, fresh fruits, canned fruits and frozen fruits. Try to figure out what has to be done to fresh pineapple to make it look like canned pineapple. Sample the two forms. Take some fresh pineapple and let it cook for awhile in a little water to see what happens. What happens if you add sweetener to the water? Wonder if other canned and fresh fruits are related. How are they treated and packaged? Read the labels on the cans to see if sugar is added.

Compare dried and fresh fruits and decide what has happened to the fruit to make it dried. Try dehydrating some apple slices by baking at a low temperature. Taste fresh fruits and their dried counterparts.

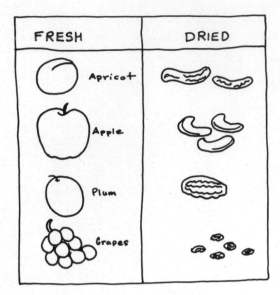

Make a chart showing pictures of fresh fruits and their dried counterparts. Include: fresh and dried apricots; prune plums and prunes; grapes and raisins; apples and dried apple slices and any others you can find. Besides dried fruits, include in your fruit chart some pictures of fruits and their other forms such as juices, sauces, and jams.

Citrus Fruit—Taste & Tell

Examine all the citrus fruits you brought back. Cut them open to notice their structure, seeds, texture and taste. Decide what things are similar among all of them and what differences they have. Can you decide why they are a family of fruits or why they are called citrus fruits? Write up a little description of each one, giving its name and distinguishing characteristics. Be sure to include how they taste. Squeeze some juice from each fruit and let the children taste a drop of juice from each one.

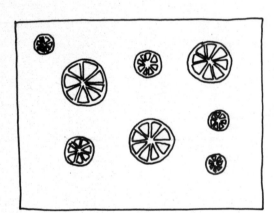

Citrus Fruit—Color Printing

Use any remaining halves of citrus fruits for printing with paints. Mix some bright-colored paints. Line paper plates or pie tins with paper towels. Pour different colors of paint on each towel so it is absorbed and can be used as a stamp pad. Dip the fruit halves in the paints and make prints on dark colored construction paper.

Grocery Store Dramatic Play

Set up a grocery store dramatic play area. Have the children bring in empty boxes, cans and other food packages. Sort them on shelves and mark prices on them. Cut the grocery ads from the newspaper to get some idea of prices. See if the children can find ads for any of the items for which you have empty packages. The children can decide on specials for the day and so forth.

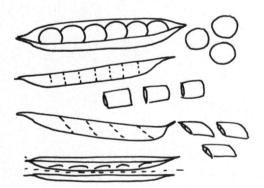

Vegetable Exploration

Bring back a batch of fresh peas and green beans. Let the children shell the peas and taste them. Try cutting the green beans as they are cut before being frozen: french-cut, sliced plain, sliced on an angle. Taste them raw. Then cook and eat them. Which way do the children like them best?

Use the empty pea pods as paint brushes if you wish.

Store Bulletin Board

Divide a bulletin board into areas and use corrugated strips of paper to represent shelves within each area. Put names over each area to correspond to the areas you visited in the store: bakery, produce, meat department, paper products and so forth. Cut out pictures of store items from magazine ads. Let the children pin them up on the bulletin board in the proper section. Encourage the children to organize the items on the shelves as they were in the store. Put one item in each area to get them started.

An Applesauce Experiment

Examine the different apples you brought back from the store. Be sure to include some golden delicious and green apples as well as the normal red ones. Are apples always red? Notice the texture, seed structure, color and taste of all the apples and decide what makes them all apples.

Cook the different kinds of apples separately and mash them up to make applesauce. Taste each kind of applesauce and see if they taste the same or different. Mix them all together to see how they taste when combined. (Rumor has it that the best applesauce is made by mixing several types of apples. Do you agree?) Add sugar or honey to part of the batch and compare the taste. Write up a little story about your applesauce experiment.

Categorizing Games

Do We Eat It Game. Make two containers (small boxes or halves of milk cartons will do). On one box draw or paste a picture of a person eating. On the other box paste the same type of picture with a big NO or X over the person. Cut out a lot of grocery products, both edible and inedible. Let the children sort them by which can be eaten and which cannot. This is a good way to talk about not tasting many poisonous or dangerous things that come from stores.

Food Sort Game. Make up master boards marked with each of the major food categories: fruits, vegetables, meat, dairy, cereals and grains. Paste a picture of a food from that category on the board. Cut out lots of food pictures and mount on cards. Children take turns picking cards and deciding on which master board it belongs.

Songs, Poems and Fingerplays

Shopping

To the tune of "Twinkle, Twinkle, Little Star"

The grocery's shelves are piled high,
Almost reaching to the sky.
Busy people hurry by,
Wondering what they should buy.
See the carts all in a row,
Through the check-out,
Out they go.

Pretend to push cart and fill it with items

At the Store

Up and down the aisles we go.
Pushing our grocery cart to and fro
Filling it up with good things to eat:
Fruits, and vegetables, cereals and meat.
Cheese and eggs and milk to drink,
And ice cream for a treat, I think.
We always buy good things galore,
Whenever we go to the grocery store.

Three Grocery Stores

A little neighborhood store

A medium sized store
And a great big supermarket,
I see.

Shall we count them?
Are you ready?
One, two, three.

Have hands for a partial rectangle shape by joining thumbs and extending fingers upward

Enlarge the shape a little
Spread hands to form a large, large shape

Repeat the three motions; indicate size of building

Five Fruits

Five different fruits at the grocery store.
Tom chose an *apple* and
now there are four.

Four different fruits we all can *see*.
Mary picked an *orange*
and that leaves three.

Three different kinds left for you.
Jeff chose a *pear*
and now there are two.

Two yummy fruits will soon be done.
Sarah took the *banana*
and now there is one.

One bunch of grapes for everyone.
We will all share them
and now there is none!

Use with felt cut-outs or pictures of fruits; children take turns eliminating each fruit as appropriate; substitute their names and the fruits they pick throughout the fingerplay

For last one use: cherries, box of berries or any fruit that comes in bunches

And more

The Grocery Store, from **Sing A Song.** Roberta McLaughlin and Lucille Wood. Prentice-Hall, 1960.

Books

Baugh, Dolores M. and Marjorie Pulsifer. **Let's Go.** Noble, 1970.

Baugh, Dolores M. and Marjorie Pulsiifer. **Supermarket.** Noble, 1970.

Bendick, Jeanne. **First Book of Supermarkets.** Watts, 1954.

Bruna, Dick. **Pappy Pig Goes to the Market.** Methuen, 1981.

Burningham, John. **The Shopping Basket.** Crowell, 1980.

Carle, Eric. **Walter the Baker.** Knopf, 1972.

Greene, Carla. **I Want to Be a Storekeeper.** Childrens Press, 1958.

Kent, Jack. **Supermarket Magic.** Random House, 1978.

Lerner, Mark. **Careers in a Supermarket.** Lerner, 1977.

Rockwell, Anne and Harlow. **The Super Market.** MacMillan, 1979.

Shannon, Terry. **About Food and Where It Comes From.** Melmont, 1961.

Schroeder, Glenn. **At the Bakery.** Melmont, 1967.

Schwartz, Alvin. **Stores.** MacMillan, 1977.

For teacher reference and use:

Buckheimer, Naomi. **Let's Take a Trip to a Bakery.** Putnam, 1956.

Uhl, Melvin John and Madeline Otteson. **How We Get Frozen Dinners.** Noble, 1965.

Wise, William. **Fresh, Canned and Frozen: Food From Past to Future.** Parents, 1971.

Hardware Store

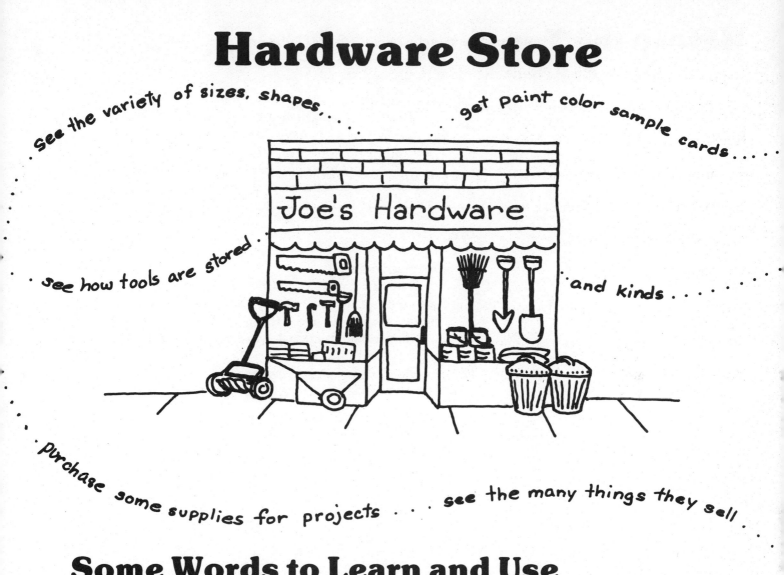

See the variety of sizes, shapes . . . . . get paint color sample cards . . . .

Joe's Hardware

see how tools are stored . . . . . . and kinds . . . .

Purchase some supplies for projects . . . see the many things they sell

Some Words to Learn and Use

nails   screws   nuts   bolts   tools   hammer   wrench

screwdriver   pliers   saw   tape measure   crowbar

pulley   wedge   lever   drill   power tools   sandpaper

lumber   pegboard   hinges   pipes   kitchen appliances

metal tubing   glass   storm windows   dowels   plugs

sockets   electric wire   door knobs   latches   locks

keys   paint   paint brush

Before the Trip / Introductory Activities

Talk About

Read the story **The Toolbox.** Ask the children where their family gets tools, what kinds of tools they have at home, and what tools they use.

Show some tools you have and talk about them.

Ask the children if animals use tools and discuss their answers. Discuss what life would be like if there were no tools.

Show and Tell

Examine blocks and select some that have rough edges and/or select some toys that need repair. Ask the children what to do about them. When they suggest fixing or sanding them, ask where we can get the things needed to fix them.

Plan to take a trip to see about getting some tools and materials used to repair toys.

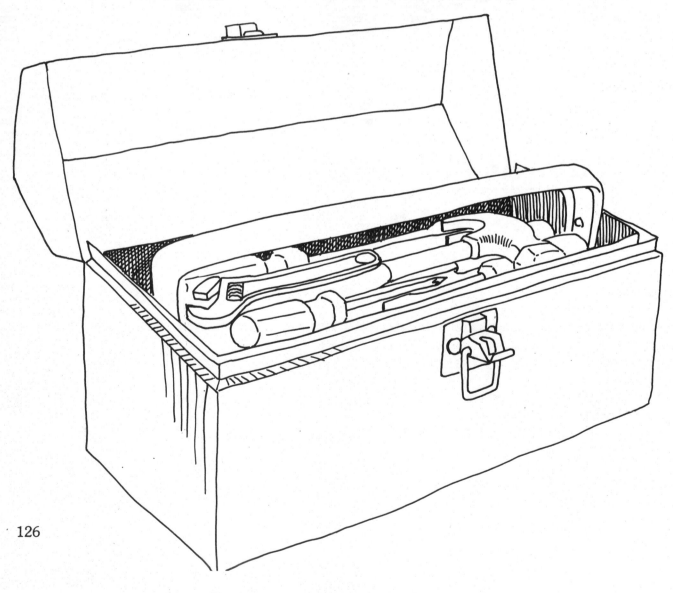

On the Trip / Ideas for Exploring

Observing

Notice the general organization of the store. Make the children aware of the categories of items in the store and how the things that are used for similar purposes are put in the same section: paint, plumbing supplies, tools, and so on.

List the many different kinds of things that are available in the store.

Browse among one section of the store at a time, noticing the tremendous variety of hardware items it contains and all the varying sizes of those items. Name and describe the uses of as many as you can.

Call attention to different types of familiar tools such as screwdrivers, hammers, wrenches.

Notice how the storage space, shelves, walls and counters are adapted to accommodate the types of items sold in the store. How are large things and small things arranged and displayed?

Point out how items are labeled. Talk about what all those fractions or inch marks on the hardware items mean.

Notice the prices of various items in the store, especially the different range of prices for some items.

If possible, watch some specialized activities in the store such as paint cans being mechanically shaken or keys being made.

Watch the way in which customer purchases are checked out and paid for. Do the clerks get items for people, or do they help themselves and take them to a central check out?

Notice any specific seasonal items the store may carry.

Counting

Count the different sizes of the same type of thing. How many sizes of nails, washers, and screws are there? How many different sizes of screwdrivers, hammers, paint brushes?

Count the different brands of the same item such as paint, mops, toasters, and irons.

Call attention to container sizes such as gallons, half-gallons, quarts of paint and other liquid items.

Speculating

Guess what some of the unfamiliar items you see might be used for. Ask the children to guess about the uses of some of the more familiar items, but ones the children may not have noticed before.

Think about what the store does with seasonal things it doesn't sell.

If the store sells toys, wonder why it does.

What would happen if the store didn't have separate spaces for all the small hardware items?

Asking

Ask the owner or clerk how they keep track of everything in the store. How do they know when they need some things?

Do they have other things you can't see, such as in a catalog?

How do they decide what something should cost or what things to put on special sales?

How do they decide what things to sell and where do they get them?

Purchasing

Buy different kinds of sandpaper to sand blocks or make sandpaper letters.

Buy some nails and/or small tools to use at the workbench.

Buy large nuts and bolts and plumbing joints to use for fit-together games.

After the Trip / Follow-up Activities

Discussion

Talk about the trip. Let the children share their experiences.

Look at hinges on cupboards and doors and talk about how they work.

Look at plumbing and other pipes at home or school and talk about their uses.

Workbench

Organize a workbench area—use different-colored cans or boxes for different-sized nails, screws, washers, and so on. Draw outlines for tools.

Obtain scrap lumber and let the children pound nails and make simple things.

Fix-it Corner

Bring in real tools and materials to use. Set up a fix-it corner to repair toys. Blocks can be sanded smooth there, puzzle pieces can be formed from plastic wood, hinges can be replaced, and loose screws tightened. Discuss the idea of recycling: fixing things instead of throwing them away.

Sandpaper

Make sandpaper letters in different grades of sandpaper.

Sand blocks using all different textures of sandpaper. Note any differences in results with the different kinds of sandpaper.

Cut bits of different sandpaper and paste on a collage with bits of smooth paper. Paint over the collage if you wish to see how the different textures absorb paint.

Feel and Tell

Place some common tools in a sack. Let each child reach in and try to describe or name a tool without looking at it. Then show the tool and discuss what kind of tool it is and what it is used for.

Fit Together

Provide a box of large nuts and bolts and let the children find ones that fit together.

Provide a box of pipes and fittings for the children to fit together.

Provide a ready-made lock box or make one yourself.

Hardware Match-ups

Make a matching game of hardware store items that are used together. The game can be made by pasting pictures of tools on one side of a master board, leaving an empty square next to it for the picture of the item that goes with it: paint brush—paint, screwdriver—screws, hammer—nails, wrench—nuts, saw—large pieces of wood, sandpaper—small rough wood, keys—locks.

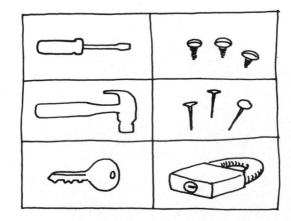

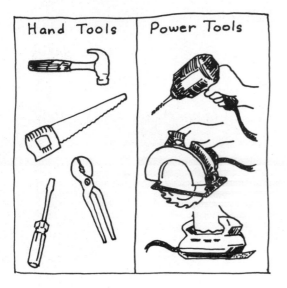

Hand Tools | Power Tools

Shades of Color Pictures

Let the children paint pictures that use shades of the same color. Use one color paint at a time and a container of water. Start at top of paper and make a stripe of paint after dipping brush in the vivid color. Dip brush in water and make another stripe. Dip in water again and paint another stripe. Repeat until paint color has gotten quite pale. The picture will produce various shades of the same color and look much like the paint sample cards. After the children understand how they can make shades of the same color by using water and paint, have them create their own designs and pictures.

What Makes it Work?

Discuss tools that are worked by hand (muscle power) and by electricity (power tools). Make a sorting game using a master board with one category for hand tools on one side and one for power tools on the other. Have the children sort pictures of tools (cut from catalogs) into the appropriate category.

Color Samples Matching Game

Using two sets of paint color samples, make a matching game for several colors. Cut the samples into individual pieces and mount four or five shades of the same color onto a 5" by 5" master board. Make separate master boards for about six different colors. Put the second set of colored pieces into a small box. Children match the pieces to the same colors on the master board. Can be used by individual children or as a small group game.

What Does it Do?

Make a categorizing game that organizes hardware store items by the functions they serve. Cut out pictures of items from Sears or hardware catalogs. Have three small containers (boxes, envelopes, or paper plates) with a picture on each that illustrates one type of category. Children sort the small cut-up pictures into the appropriate container. This game would be done with an adult at first. Some samples of categories would be:

Things that cut: All types of shears, saws, scissors, utility knives.

Things that hold things together: Nails, screws, nuts, bolts, hinges.

Things that make things smoother: Sanders, polishers, sandpaper, file, rasp.

Songs, Poems and Fingerplays

To the tune of "Mulberry Bush"

Make hammering motions

Make sanding motions

Make sawing motions

This is the Way

This is the way we hammer a nail,
Hammer a nail, hammer a nail.
This is the way we hammer a nail,
So early in the morning.

This is the way we sand our blocks . . .
So early in the morning.

This is the way we saw our wood . . .
So early in the morning.

The Tool Song

Did you ever see a hammer
Pound this way and that way
And this way and that way,
Did you ever see a hammer
Pound this way and that?

Did you ever see a saw
Cut this way and that way
And this way and that way,
Did you ever see a saw
Cut this way and that?

(Add other tools and the accompanying
motions)

To the tune of "Did You Ever See a Lassie?"

*Children imitate up and down pounding motions
with wrists*

Imitate sawing motions with arm

Imitate pounding

Imitate turning
Imitate uses of each tool

The Tools

I have a little hammer
That can pound nails all the day;
And a funny little monkey wrench
Than can turn things any way.
There's a measure, a screwdriver
And a saw too.
Is there anything you'd like me
To fix for you?

131

Johnny Works With One Hammer

Traditional

Johnny works with one hammer,
One hammer, one hammer,
Johnny works with one hammer   *Make pounding motion with one fist*
All day long.

Susie works with two hammers,   *Add pounding motion with second fist*
Two hammers, two hammers,   *Continue up to five hammers; after fists add feet,*
Susie works with two hammers,   *one at a time, and head for the pounding motions;*
All day long.   *vary the names as you start each verse, and have*
                                   that child start the motion

(Last verse:)

Robin works with five hammers,
Five hammers, five hammers,   *All parts making hammering motions.*
Robin works with five hammers,
Now he puts them down.   *Stop all motions*

And more

The Grocery Store from **Sing a Song.** Lucille Wood and Roberta MacLaughlin. Prentice Hall, 1960. For a hardware store change words to read "hardware store" and various items purchased at that store.

Hammer, Hammer, Hammer, The Carpenter, from **Finger Frolics.** Liz Cromwell and Dixie Hibner. Partner, 1976.

Books

Beim, Jerrold. **Tim and the Tool Chest.** Morrow, 1951.

Gibbons, Gail. **Tool Book.** Holiday, 1982.

Homan, Dianne. **In Christina's Toolbox.** Lollipop Power, 1981.

Kesselman, Judi R. **I Can Use Tools.** Elsevier Science, 1982.

Leavitt, J. **The True Book of Tools for Building.** Childrens Press, 1961.

Rockwell, Anne. **Toolbox.** MacMillan, 1971.

Schwartz, Alvin. **Stores.** MacMillan, 1977.

Weisenthal, Ted and Eleanor. **Let's Find Out About Tools.** Watts, 1969.

Zaffo, George. **Giant Nursery Book of Things That Work.** Doubleday, 1967.

Hospital

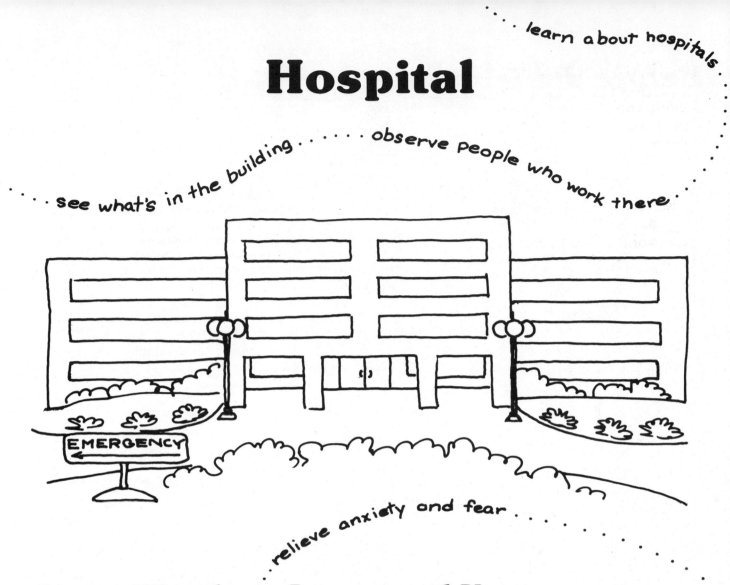

learn about hospitals

observe people who work there

see what's in the building

relieve anxiety and fear

Some Words to Learn and Use

doctor intern resident nurse aide name tag

receptionist volunteer technician patient

waiting room gift shop admitting office

emergency room elevator ambulance siren

wheel chair litter laboratory blood pressure

thermometer stethoscope stitches cast operation

adjustable beds nursery X-ray pharmacy pills

medicine sterilize ward tray dietician

physical therapy anesthetic oxygen tank scanner

Before the Trip / Introductory Activities

PLEASE NOTE: Children's experiences with hospitals are apt to be of a sudden nature, involving their own emergency needs or those of a parent who may disappear to a "strange place." In such cases, prior educational experience can be enormously helpful to the child. Many hospitals have special tours for preschool children. If this service is available, do take advantage of it. Call well in advance as space fills up very quickly. If your community does not offer this service, plan to visit the hospital anyway and explore the public areas, conducting your own tour using the following suggestions. Your example will model the importance of this experience to hospital staff. Also try to work with volunteer services of your hospital to establish a tour program for children.

Talk About

Ask if anyone has been to the hospital and what they did or saw there. Let the children share their knowledge and experience about hospitals. Find out if any parents have been to the hospital or work in hospitals and discuss that information. If parents have been in the hospital, ask what happened to the parent at the hospital and what they said about it. Also discuss the feelings the children had while their parents were in the hospital.

Ask the children who works in hospitals. If they mention doctors and nurses, ask where else they see doctors and nurses. Talk about some differences between the doctor's office, a clinic, and the hospital. Explain that hospitals see outpatients, just like an office or a clinic, but they also have inpatients who have to stay in the hospital for a few days.

Read

Read the story **Curious George Goes to the Hospital.** Talk about Curious George's adventures at the hospital and wonder which things in the book would really be found at the hospital. Plan to go and see. Ask the children if a monkey would go to a hospital. If the children wonder about that, plan to ask at the hospital.

On the Trip / Ideas for Exploring

Observing

Look around outside at the entrance to the building. Notice if there are several entrances and if one is an emergency or ambulance entrance. How is it set up to offer easy access to the building? Are there any special signs or clues that tell you this is a hospital?

Notice any special equipment near the entrance area or emergency room that might be needed to assist people. Are there wheel chairs, litters, oxygen tanks, portable X-ray machines, or blood pressure measurement devices on wheels?

Look at the lobby area and waiting rooms. Is there a large and small lobby, special waiting room by the business office, emergency room, outpatient area, as well as a main lobby area? How are they all decorated? Are some nicer than others? Notice the furniture, plants, or other decorative touches. Are there plaques, special tributes or names engraved on walls anywhere honoring people who have been involved with the hospital?

What other areas do you see in the general lobby section of the hospital? Is there a gift shop, coffee shop, reception area, chapel, business office, telephone operator, elevator, directory or map of the hospital?

Walk down the corridors of the hospital and notice their composition. Are the floors easy to care for and very clean? Do you see anything special along the walls such as mirrors, loud speakers, dumb waiters or systems for sending information or medicines from one area to another? Are there many glass-enclosed areas with hospital personnel visible inside?

Notice special features in some halls or offices such as the doctors' call board, X-ray viewing boxes mounted on walls, clip boards and charts, flip cardex files of patients in the hospital, plants or other items to be delivered to patients.

Observe the people working in the hospital. Do they wear special clothes, name tags, or coats that indicate their department or the work they do? Do you see any people who are patients either arriving or leaving the hospital? Do you see doctors or nurses working with patients in some way?

Notice any food being served in the hospital. Are there big carts with stacks of trays on them?

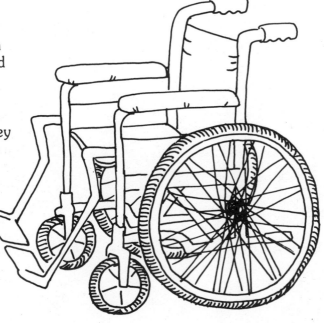

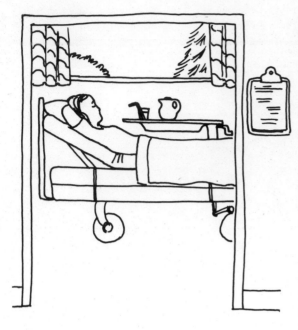

Asking

Ask the receptionist to show you how a record is kept of who is in the hospital and where their room is located. Ask how the plants and other items get delivered to the patients.

What duties does the receptionist have? Are there passes to give to visitors or special visiting hours to monitor?

Ask the telephone operator to show you how the doctors' call board and the paging system in the hospital work. Do all the announcements over the public address system come from the same cental area, or can anyone talk on the system from anyplace in the hospital?

Ask the people in the gift shop to tell you about their work. Are they volunteers helping to raise money for the hospital by the gift shop sales? What items do people buy most frequently? Talk about the types of things they sell in the gift shop, and who decides what things they will carry in the gift shop.

Ask people in the emergency room area to explain some of the equipment you see. What are things called, and what do the various machines do? Ask to see an X-ray clipped up on the lighted viewing box. Perhaps someone can explain what part of the body is visible in the X-ray.

Ask to see the food service area or how food is served to people in the hospital. Do people get to choose what they want? How do patients know what they can have to eat? Who prepares the meals and who decides which patients can have what? Perhaps you can see sample menus. Do they have special menus for children?

Ask for demonstrations on adjustable hospital beds, self-guiding wheel chairs, and adjustable litters. Let the children notice all the different items on wheels and the sizes of the wheels.

Sensing

Listen to the sounds of the hospital. Do you hear continual sounds over the public address system? What are they saying and how do they sound? Do you hear any sirens, noises from the TV sets, conversations? Is the overall atmosphere quiet with some intruding noises?

What smells do you notice in the hospital? Are there smells from cleaning, disinfectant and sanitizing, medicine and food? Do different areas of the hospital have different aromas?

Talk about how it might feel to come to the hospital in an emergency. Talk about feeling scared or worried about what might happen along with the physical problem of pain or sickness that brought you there.

Collecting

Bring back anything you can from the trip. Collect any free tongue depressors, tubes from syringes, syringes, samples of bandages, surgical masks, gloves and so on.

Take pictures of the children at the hospital to use after the trip.

After the Trip / Follow-up Activities

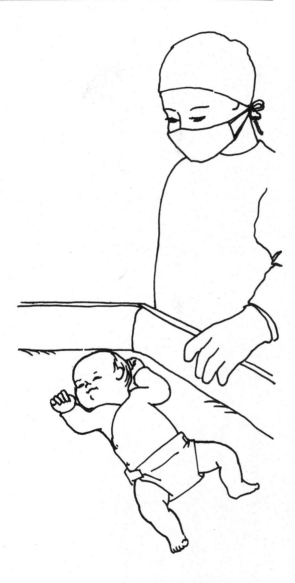

Discussion

Let the children talk about the trip. Encourage discussion in groups and on an individual basis. Be sure you are hearing all their comments and concerns. Generate several lists based on their comments. These should include: things we learned about the hospital, questions we still wonder about, our feelings about going to the hospital (for ourselves or others).

Talk about cheering people up when they are not feeling well, as Curious George did in the story. Think about what you could do to cheer up some children who might be in the hospital. Plan to send some things to the hospital such as pictures, homemade floral decorations and perhaps some homemade games or books about your trip.

Talk about reasons why people go to the hospital: to have an operation, a baby, or a cast put on, or to get stitches. Talk about anesthetics and how they are used to help people not feel the pain of some procedures.

Look over the items you brought back and discuss them. Explain why surgical masks and gloves are worn. Look over the syringes and talk about their uses. Explain that syringes and needles are used for many different things: to draw blood for blood tests; to give medicine; to give local anesthetics so people won't feel something that might hurt; to give inoculations to prevent diseases. Read the book **No Measles, No Mumps For Me** to explain inoculations.

Medical Instruments Chart

Look over those diagrams of body systems and talk about how they work. Talk about things that happen to our body and cause us problems such as infections, cuts, or fractures. What does the doctor do to find out what the problem is and how to treat it? Make a chart that shows what various medical instruments measure, and what the

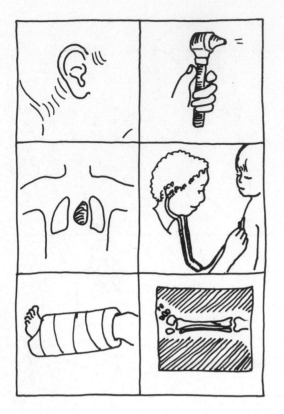

treatment might be. (Use pictures cut out from throw-away medical magazines available from any doctor or hospital which have lots of ads in them.)

Body System and Problems	How to Measure	Treatment
Circulatory— Heart Trouble	Stethoscope, EKG, take pulse	Rest, medicine, oxygen, diets
Infection	Thermometer, blood tests (for virus)	Rest, medicine, shot
High blood pressure	Blood pressure cuff	Medicine, low-salt diet
Respiratory— Sore throat, cold, ear infection, pneumonia	Thermometer, blood tests, otoscope, X-ray	Rest, medicine, shots
Skeletal— Broken bones	X-ray	Cast
Digestive— Stomach ache	X-ray, examination	Rest, medicine, shot

and so on. Talk about the fact that some illnesses like flu can affect more than one system. Also notice that some tests such as blood tests and X-rays can be used to look for many different problems.

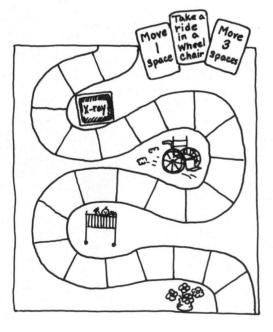

Make a Hospital Board Game

On a large piece of tagboard, trace a path and mark off spaces along the path. Draw special symbols by some spaces to indicate places or procedures seen in the hospital. Make a set of playing cards to use with the board. Children will pick the cards which will indicate how to move along the path. Most cards will say "Move 1, 2 or 3 spaces," but some will have special pictures indicating the player has to go to the appropriate space. Examples for special cards: "Ride in wheel chair," "Buy gift in gift shop," "Go to business office," "Visit babies in nursery," "Have X-ray taken." For each of the special cards the player stays on the spot for one turn. Use spools with faces drawn on them for players.

Made up Stories

Make up stories about situations involving a hospital. If you wish, let the children dramatize some of the stories.

Dramatic Play

Set up a hospital dramatic play area. Doll beds can become hospital beds. Other surfaces can be covered with towels to look like examining tables or storage space for medical kit materials and items brought back from the hospital. Ask any parents from the health field if they have any supplies to contribute to your hospital corner. (One program had a parent contribute a cast for a large Raggedy Ann doll's leg.) Large cardboard tubes can be used to make pretend casts. Paint them white if you want them to look more realistic. Children can pretend to be doctors, nurses, patients, office personnel, telephone operators, visitors, volunteers and a variety of people observed on your trip.

Book and Materials Display

Put out several hospital-related books for the children to look at. Also put out books with pictures of the body and diagrams of all its systems: respiratory, circulatory, skeletal, and so on. Encyclopedias often have good colored diagrams (with overlays) of the human body. Science museums, pharmaceutical houses, or toy libraries may have body parts models you can borrow to add to your display. Include some X-rays and hospital-related play equipment in the display for children to look at and manipulate.

Read and discuss several of the books and explain any of the other materials in the display. Be sure to answer any of the children's questions about items on display.

Body Systems Diagram

After talking about systems of our body and some of the internal organs, let the children make a body diagram/collage using various materials to represent organs and systems. Paste items on a torso shape cut from tagboard. Some possibilities are: thin spaghetti for bones, pieces of sponge for lungs, kidney beans for kidneys, a heart candy or lima bean for the heart, elbow macaroni for small intestines, large macaroni or rigatoni for large intestines, thin red licorice for circulatory systems (arteries, veins), clusters of raisins, dried prunes, or a sponge for the brain, straight macaroni for esophagus, small balloon for stomach and bladder, steel wool for muscles.

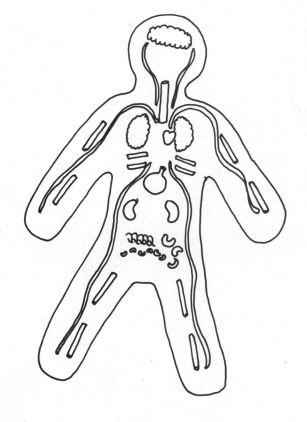

Songs, Poems and Fingerplays

To the Hospital

This is the way we go to the hospital
Go to the hospital
Go to the hospital
This is the way we go to the hospital
If we are sick in the morning.

(Additional verses:)

This is the way we wait at the hospital . . .

This is the way they take our pulse . . .

This is the way they check our blood . . .

This is the way they hear our heart . . .

This is the way they take an X-ray . . .

This is the way they put on a cast . . .

To the tune of "Mulberry Bush"

Pretend to drive to hospital

Children sit and make fidgety and wiggling movements

Put fingers of one hand on wrist of other hand

Pretend to prick finger

Put on pretend stethoscope and move it around

Pretend to take picture

Pretend to wrap up leg

To the tune of "This Old Man"

This Little Child

This little child, he felt sick,
Drove to the hospital—quick, quick, quick,
They checked his ears and throat and head,
And sent him home to go to bed!

This little child, broke her toe,
Oh my dear, it hurt her so,
Rushed to the hospital, X-rayed the little bone
Taped it up and sent her home.

This little child had a pain,
What it was, was not so plain,
They did some tests so they could tell
What medicine would make him well.

At the Hospital

I went to the hospital and what did I see?
I saw some babies looking at me.
The littlest babies, all nice and new,
Sleeping and eating is what they do.

A Hospital Trip

I like to ride in a wheel chair
And turn it round and round.   *Pretend to work wheel chair with hands*
I like to take the elevator
And ride it up and down.   *Stretch up and bend down*
I like to see the flowers and toys
They have in the gift shop,   *Pretend to smell flowers or play with stuffed animal*
But there's one thing I do not like,
That's when I get a shot! Ouch!   *Children pretend to give themselves a shot*

A Hospital Bed

Have children lie down flat on floor A hospital bed can do some tricks.
Children raise and lower heads   It moves up and down by a button that flicks,
Lift heads off floor   It's head goes up,
Lift feet too   It's feet do too,
Sit all the way up   It's amazing what that bed can do!

Four Little Babies

Four little babies in the nursery I see,   *Hold up four fingers*
The nurse gives one to a mommy
And now there are three.   *Hold up three fingers*

Three little babies crying boo hoo,
The nurse picks up one
And now there are two.   *Hold up two fingers*

Two little babies cooing for fun,
Along comes a daddy
And now there is one.   *Hold up one finger*

One little baby is all that I can see,
But that is the one for my family.   *Pretend to rock baby*

Books

Bemelmans, Ludwig. **Madeline.** Simon & Schuster, 1939.

Breinburg, Petronella. **Doctor Shawn.** Crowell, 1974.

Bruna, Dick. **Miffy in the Hospital.** Metheun, 1976.

Clark, Betinna and Lester Coleman. **Going to the Hospital.** Random House, 1971.

Collier, James Lincoln. **Danny Goes to the Hospital.** Norton, 1970.

Elliott, Ingrid. **Hospital Roadmap.** Resources Children, 1982.

Greene, Carla. **Doctors and Nurses: What Do They Do?** Harper & Row, 1963.

Marina, Barbara Pavis. **Eric Needs Stitches.** Addison-Wesley, 1979.

Pope, Billy N., and Romana Emmons. **Your World: Let's Visit the Hospital.** Taylor, 1968.

Rey, Margret and H. A. **Curious George Goes to the Hospital.** Houghton-Mifflin, 1966.

Rockwell, Harlan. **My Doctor.** MacMillan, 1973.

Shay, Arthur. **What Happens When You Go to the Hospital.** Contemporary Books, 1969.

Showers, Paul. **No Measles, No Mumps for Me.** Crowell, 1980.

Showers, Paul. **A Drop of Blood.** Crowell, 1967.

Showers, Paul. **Hear Your Heart.** Crowell, 1968.

Sobol, Harriet L. **Jeff's Hospital Book.** Walck, 1975.

Steedman, Julie. **Emergency Room.** Windy Hill, 1974.

Stein, Sara Bonnet. **A Hospital Story.** Walker, 1974.

Stone, Bernard. **Emergency Mouse.** Prentice-Hall, 1978.

Tamburine, Jean. **I Think I Will Go to the Hospital.** Abingdon, 1965.

Weber, Alfons. **Elizabeth Gets Well.** Crowell, 1970.

Wolde, Gunilla. **Betsy and the Doctor.** Random House, 1978.

Ziegler, Sandra. **At the Hospital—A Surprise for Krissy.** Childs World, 1976.

For teacher reference & use:

Howe, James. **The Hospital Book.** Crown, 1981.

Lumber Yard / Building Center

learn about lumber--how it's stored--how it's cut and used--how much it costs--different kinds

collect wood samples, wood shavings (curls), and sawdust

see other building materials

Some Words to Learn and Use

lumber   board   plank   plywood   veneer   two-by-four

paneling   unfinished   prefinished   stain   cupboards

cabinets   hinges   handles   molding   millwork

woodwork   trim   formica   sink   door   stair tread

beam   carpet   tile   linoleum   wallpaper   railing

window frame   wallboard   masonite   pegboard   lathe

plane   sawdust   siding   hardwood   softwood   grain

knot   rough   smooth   post   forklift   maple   pine

oak

Before the Trip / Introductory Activities

Talk About

Look around your own room or a kitchen area and notice the cabinets and wood items like doors and woodwork in the rooms. Ask the children where those items came from. Were they already made or did someone build them? Plan to go someplace where you might find wood to use for building or cabinets which have already been built.

Show and Tell

Look up lumber, forest, and forest products in an encyclopedia and show the children the pictures of large trees, the logs cut from the trees, and how they are transported. Look for pictures of sawmills where logs are converted to board lumber or thin veneers. Show the children any pictures of the lumber being transported to the lumberyard. Ask if they would like to see where the boards are now.

On the Trip / Ideas for Exploring

Observing

Notice the stacks of lumber and the various sizes and shapes it comes in. Think about what the different types of lumber might be used for. Name as many different kinds as you can.

Look for other building materials that are available. Do you see wood trim materials, cabinets, concrete blocks, bricks, roofing materials, linoleum, ceiling tile, carpet, prefinished paneling, wallpaper, or other items? Are there samples people can take home to help them decide what they want? Point out the different materials by name and ask the children if they have seen materials like these in their homes or schools.

Is there a work area with saws where lumber is being cut? If possible, watch this process and notice the pile of sawdust and wood curls accumulating on the floor.

Could you observe a forklift truck moving stacks of lumber? If not, wonder how the lumber gets moved, first onto the shelves and later onto the delivery trucks.

Asking

Ask the salespeople to explain something about the different kinds of lumber and what they are used for. Can they tell you about plywood, wood veneers, and different types and grades of woodboards they might sell? Can they tell you about hard and soft wood and what that means?

Ask someone to tell you about the cost of different kinds of lumber. Are some woods more expensive than others?

Can they tell you how various types of wood trims are made? Do they do any of that work on the premises?

Ask someone to tell you about the work they do at the lumber yard. Do they cut wood to size for special orders? do they make roof beams or cabinets or other items? If not, do they take orders and have them made someplace else?

How do they deliver the lumber? What machines do they use to help in their work? Can they show them to you, if you haven't already observed them in action?

Comparing

Look closely at the unfinished wood and notice the different grains and textures. Being careful to avoid splinters, touch the woods and see if they feel different: smooth, rough, hard or soft. In what other ways do

woods differ? Compare the grains and decide which ones look most interesting.

Compare unfinished and prefinished wood.

If prefinished paneling is on display, notice the grains in the panels and decide whether the grain shows up more before or after the wood is finished.

If small samples of finished woods are available, take them over to the unfinished wood stacks and see if you can recognize and match the grains.

Take along a tape measure and measure the different sizes of lumber. Measure in each direction so you can decide what one-by-four or two-by-four means. Ask the salesperson to help explain how lumber is measured and sold.

Measure other building materials as well: the concrete blocks, floor tiles, ceiling tiles, doors, window frames and others. Talk about why measuring might be important in building.

Collecting

Ask for small samples of any construction materials and pieces of wood to take back for various projects. Ask the salesperson to tell you what type each piece of wood is. Write it on the wood someplace.

Bring a large container and ask to fill it with sawdust to take back with you. Also collect any of those wood curls you see lying around.

If the yard will cut the lumber for you, buy a hard wood two-by-four and have it cut into two-foot long sections.

After the Trip / Some Things to Do

Discussion

Let the children tell you the things they remember from the trip. Using the children's comments, make a list entitled "Things We Learned About Lumber and Building Materials."

Ask the children to tell you about things they noticed in their homes or at school that remind them of things seen on the trip.

All About Lumber Bulletin Board or Poster

Design a bulletin board or poster that tells about lumber and how it is used. Start with the two types of trees (see Tree Walk) and add pictures of plain lumber and then the things made from lumber.

Conifers or evergreen trees such as pines, fir, hemlock, spruce, cedar and redwood produce lumber called softwood. Softwood is used for siding, posts, planks, beams, doors, frames, panels, wood trim, and boxes.

Deciduous trees such as maple, oak, birch, poplar, aspen, beech and walnut produce lumber called hardwood. Mahogany, ebony, teak and rosewood are tropical hardwoods. Hardwood lumber is used for furniture, paneling, flooring, baseball bats and tool handles, and musical instruments like guitars. Pieces of hardwood can be used for parts of furniture.

Sample Matching

See if you can find things in your room that look like the samples you collected on your trip. Do you have molding, door frames, or trim that look like the samples? If you brought back formica samples, see if they match anything in your room.

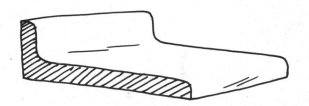

Wood Shavings

Collect samples of different woods and try planing them. Do the wood shavings look the same or different? Collect the wood shavings from each sample in a plastic bag and examine them to notice differences in color, size, texture and so on. After you have finished examining the wood shavings, they can be used as hair for paper bag or paper plate puppets. Small bits of wood can be painted and used for features in the puppets.

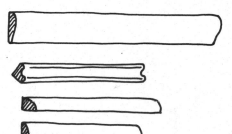

Woodworking Area

Set up a workbench or woodworking area. Provide saws, hammers and nails. With supervision, let the children saw wood and use it to build simple things. As you and the children work with the wood, decide if it is hard or soft. Check the name of the wood sample to see if your guesses were correct.

Set up an area for painting and staining wood. Use some light and dark stains as well as one and two coats of paint. What do you observe about how finishing changes the wood? Which finish allows you to see more of the wood grain? Which one do you like best? For younger children, use plain water and water colors brushed onto the wood.

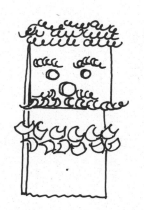

147

Woodcuts and Prints

Use small wood scraps of different shapes for printing. They can be used to make homemade wrapping paper.

Wood blocks to use for printing, or simple woodcut pictures can be made by making indentations in soft wood. Using the point of a scissors or pen, make a design pattern on the wood. Cover with a tempera paint. Place a small piece of paper over the block and press gently so that it picks up the print. Since paint will not have stuck to the indented areas, they will remain clear to reveal the design.

Block Area

Look at your blocks and see if the children can figure out how they relate to the lumber you have just seen. Take out the two-foot long pieces of wood and decide what you need to do to turn them into blocks. Measure the sizes you want, saw, sand and stain the wood for your own homemade blocks. Add to your other blocks.

Turn your block area into a dramatic play lumber yard. Measure the size of the blocks, organize them by size and put signs up to tell the board length. Children can come and purchase blocks with play money and have them delivered to a place in the room to use for building.

Wood Products Sorting Games

Have the children cut out from magazines, newspaper ads and catalogs all sorts of pictures of wood products. These should include everything from wood toys to pictures of paneling and cabinets. Use the pictures to play a variety of games sorting them into different categories to illustrate certain concepts such as:

- Things we can buy at a lumber yard and things we can't buy there.
- Things we use for building houses and things we just use for living or playing.
- Things our parents would buy and use and things we would use.
- Things that are finished products and things we need to finish ourselves.

Each concept creates a different game. Different sorting boxes or master boards can be made and used, or the pictures could be used in small group discussions and sorted by the group as a whole.

How a Tree Becomes a Block

Make up your own picture book telling the story of lumber. Collect pictures illustrating trees in forests, lumberjacks or loggers cutting them down, logs being transported to the sawmill, sawmills in operation, lumber being transferred to lumberyards and the two-by-four you bought and had cut up. Have the children dictate comments to go with each picture. Put them together into your own book. Collect any pictures the lumber yard may have, and take some of your own.

Sawdust Modeling Material

Mix five cups sawdust with one cup wheat paste and four-five cups water. Shape material around a foundation, such as a styrofoam ball, or puppet head. Allow several days to dry, then paint. This lightweight material can be used in a variety of modeling projects such as paperweights, decorative ornaments, busts or statues of favorite animals or people or other gifts made by children.

Wood and Glue

Glue several curlicues of wood together to see what happens. Talk about how plywood is made by gluing several thin strips of wood veneer together. Try staining your own homemade bits of plywood.

Glue a thin curlicue of wood onto a thicker piece of wood to explain how a veneer of one type of wood is added to another. Think about when and why people would make and use wood that had a veneered finish.

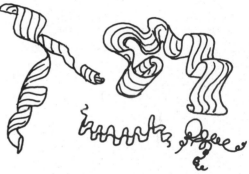

Songs, Poems and Fingerplays

To the tune of "I'm a Little Teapot"

Hands curved over heads to form a tree
Pretend to cut down tree
Pretend to lift and load on trucks and drive off
Spread hands wide apart to indicate long boards

The Lumber Song

First you find a tree that's big and tall,
Watch the lumberjack make it fall.
Off to the sawmill the logs will go
And turn into boards that look just so.

The Lumber Store

Wooden boards called two-by-fours,
Wooden cabinets and doors,
Wood for walls and stairs and floors,
Paint for fences and so much more,
We will find at the lumber store.

Trees and Wood

Each tree is very special,
And has a special name.
And when it turns to lumber,
Its name will stay the same.
The pine trees give us knotty pine,
That's used for walls or doors.
The oak tree gives us solid oak
For tables, chairs or floors.

Wood We Use

The trees that grow in forests
Where people camp and play,
Will someday be so many things
That we use every day.

Have children think of things they use that are made of wood

Sawdust

Children imitate sawing

Point to floor
Scoop up and make mixing motions

Buzz—Buzz—Buzz, the saw works so hard
Cutting up the boards at the lumber yard.
Little mounds of sawdust are piling up high.
We'll take some home and mix it,
To use by and by.

And more

The Wood Chopper, from **Rhymes for Fingers and Flannelboards.** Louise Binder Scott and
J. J. Thompson. McGraw-Hill, 1960.

Books

Brown, Marcia. **All Butterflies.** Atheneum, 1974.

Emberley, Barbara. **Story of Paul Bunyan.** Prentice-Hall, 1963.

Green, Carla. **I Want to Be a Carpenter.** Childrens Press, 1959.

Kay, Helen. **Apron On, Apron Off.** Scholastic, 1972.

Kelly, Karin. **Carpentry.** Lerner, 1974.

Kurelek, William. **Lumberjack.** Houghton-Mifflin, 1974.

Mitgutsch, Ali. **From Tree to Table.** Carolrhoda, 1981.

Newton, James R. **Forest Log.** Harper & Row, 1980.

Scary, Richard. **What Do People Do All Day?** Random House, 1968.

Thelen, Gerda. **The Toy Maker.** Whitman, 1935.

Wade, Harlan. **Wood.** Raintree, 1979.

For teacher reference and use:

Michaelson, M. **Firewood—A Woodcutter's Fieldguide to Trees in Summer and Winter.** Minn. Scholarly.

Restaurant

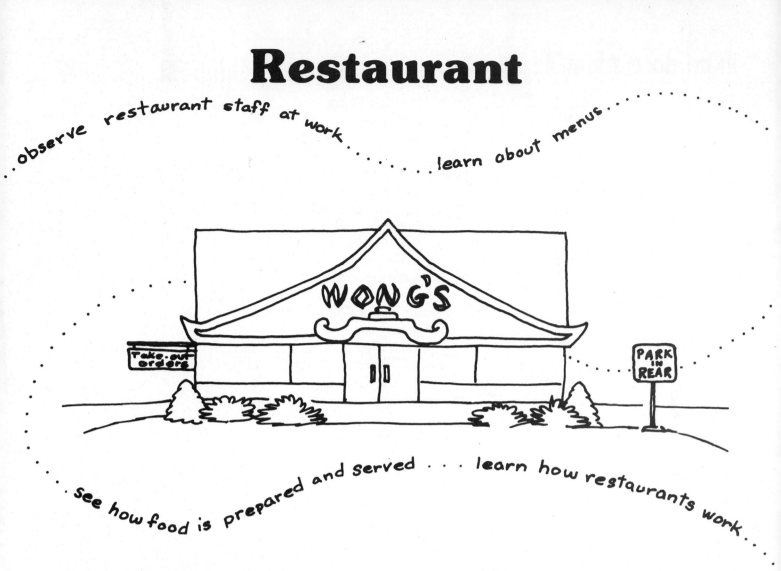

...observe restaurant staff at work......learn about menus...

...see how food is prepared and served...learn how restaurants work...

Some Words to Learn and Use

menu   waitress   waiter   hostess   maitre d'   chef

salad bar   booth   counter   place setting   placemat

tablecloth   centerpiece   busboy   cafeteria   fast-food

family-style   uniform   entree   a la carte   beverage

dessert   appetizer   dining room   grill   order   tip

check   powder room   award   seafood   cafe

coffee shop   buffet   take-out   drive-thru   gourmet

ethnic

Talk About

Ask the children if they have eaten at any restaurants. Make a list of the ones they mention and let them tell you their favorites. Talk about the different kinds of restaurants they mention. Are they fast-food, family-style, or restaurants featuring foods of a specific nationality?

Think of the kinds of foods the children have eaten in the restaurants you have listed. Wonder how those foods are prepared. Do they prepare a few things very quickly using special equipment (as in fast food restaurants), or do they have a full kitchen and cook things to order?

Generate a list of questions from the children about how foods are purchased and prepared in the restaurant. Plan to ask those questions on the trip.

Please note: Many fast-food restaurants have special tours available for preschool groups. Plan to take advantage of the resource, but plan also to visit a different type of restaurant for comparison. The follow-up activities would be appropriate for use with any type of restaurant trip.

On the Trip / Ideas for Exploring

Observing

Notice if the building that houses the restaurant is unique or if it looks just like several others of the same type. Is it part of a chain with special identifying characteristics? Notice the color of the roof, style of construction, shape of the building and so on.

Are there any construction features that suggest a particular ethnic identification for this restaurant? Does its appearance suggest a particular type of restaurant such as a fancy supper club or a truck stop? Talk about what gives the building this special appearance.

Notice the area around the building and how it is adapted for the needs of the restaurant. Is there parking space, a special drive-up arrangement, an identifying sign and so on?

Notice the entryway into the restaurant. Do you come right into the table area, or is there some kind of lobby or reception area? Notice what's in that area. Do you seat yourself, or is there someone to take you to your table? How do you know what to do when you enter? Are there signs, or does the building's style tell you?

Are there booths, tables and counters, or just tables? Are there special settings on the tables? Notice the type of table setting. Does it look plain or fancy? Do they use paper placemats, tablecloths, or nothing? What things are on the tables such as salt and pepper shakers, napkin holders, ashtrays, sugar bowl, any kind of centerpiece? How do the things on the tables contribute to the restaurant's appearance?

Notice the lighting in the room and what effect it has on the atmosphere. Is it bright daylight or dark? What makes it that way? Is there a bar? Does that look the same as the rest of the restaurant? Are there room dividers for different areas?

Notice the way in which the room is decorated: floor covering, wall covering, lighting fixtures, decorations on the wall and so on. Are there plants or other decorations that contribute to the atmosphere? Notice the type of tables and chairs. Is there a salad bar or cases that display desserts or special food items? Are there pictures of any foods to tempt you? Name and identify all the different things you see in the room.

Notice the clothes the people who work there are wearing. Do their clothes tell you anything about their jobs? Are all the people wearing the same kinds of uniforms? Does the style or type of uniform worn contribute in any way to the atmosphere in the

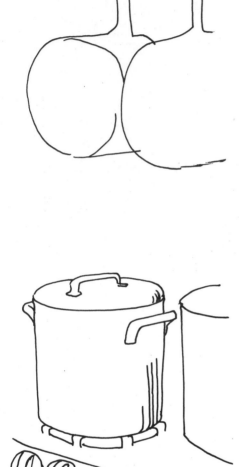

restaurant? Talk about the types of jobs people do in restaurants and use the names for those positions.

Observe the people at work. How do the tables get cleared and reset? How is the food carried to the tables? Is it a self-service or cafeteria style restaurant, or does someone take your order and bring the food and drinks to your table? Do you see any signs of food preparation, or is it all done in a kitchen area? Can you see where the kitchen is?

Look at the menus. Are they plain or fancy? Is it a long menu with many different things on it, or is it a short piece of paper? Are there pictures on the menu or funny or special names for things? Is there a children's menu also? Look at the way the menu is organized and talk about the different sections of the menu which list things by courses, such as appetizers, main courses, desserts, beverages, and so on. Talk about the meanings of words like "a la carte," "complete" or "full course dinner." Point out the prices for different items.

Observe customers getting their checks and paying their bills. Notice if they leave money on the table. Talk about tips or gratuities and what that means. How do the customers pay their bills? Does the waitress take the money or credit card, or does the customer pay a cashier?

Asking

Ask the receptionist or cashier to show the children the cash register and explain how they ring things up. Also ask about credit cards and how they deal with those kinds of charges.

Ask the waitress to show you an order book and the system for conveying orders to the kitchen. How do they know when an order is ready?

Ask to see the service and supply areas and how the dishes are bussed. How are supplies maintained and what system does this restaurant use? Are there individual stations with silverware, dishes, and napkins for specific areas, or is there one central supply area? How does that work, and who keeps stocking the supply areas? Who fills pitchers, sugar bowls, coffee pots and so on?

Ask to see the kitchen and ask about how the food is prepared. How is the kitchen organized? Are there special areas of the kitchen for different items such as a salad area where all salads are prepared? Who does the cooking? Are things cooked to order or reheated? How do they keep from getting in each other's way? Who is in charge? How is food ordered and who does that? Ask all the questions you had prepared in advance. Ask to see any refrigerators, freezers and stoves, as well as their pots and pans. How does this kitchen compare to a home kitchen? Notice the clothes worn by people in the kitchen area and any signs of special health practices used in the kitchen. Do they wear or use any special things to help keep things sanitary?

Counting

Count the tables and number of seats at the tables. Estimate how many people the restaurant can serve at any one time. Notice the different-sized tables and any arrangements for expanding tables to hold larger parties. Count the number of tables for parties of two, four and larger groups. Which size table do they have the most of? Count the number of booths and seats at any counters as well.

Count how many people work in the restaurant, the number of different jobs, and the number of people in each job.

Count the number of items on the menu in each of the sections. Which things do they have the most of?

Count light fixtures, the number of rooms in the restaurant, and any other architectural features that lend themselves to counting such as windows or doors.

Count how many high chairs or booster seats they have. Wonder what would happen if they ran out. Make some guesses about whether this restaurant serves many families with children based on how many children's seats you see.

Collecting

Take back as many things as they will give you such as the order books, sample placemats, menus and/or children's menus, paper chef or kitchen hats, plastic mitts or hair nets (if they use them).

Take pictures to use later. If possible, photograph the kitchen and table areas of the restaurant and the personnel who work there.

Sensing

Notice all the smells in the restaurant. Can you recognize any of the particular smells such as coffee, chocolate, hamburgers on a grill, or bread baking? Identify as many different aromas as you can. Are there any ones that dominate?

Be aware of the different textures in the environment. Is it a hard, smooth, plastic environment, or a warm wood and soft texture environment?

Is the feeling of the place very busy and hectic, or

calm and relaxing? Are you aware of people smiling?

Listen to the noises of the restaurant. Do you hear people chattering and laughing, dishes clattering, water pouring, food sizzling, fire crackling? What other sounds are you aware of?

Where do all the sensations come from? Are you aware of noises or activities outside the restaurant as well, or does the outside world seem far away?

After the Trip / Follow-up Activities

Discussion

Talk about the trip and write down all the children's impressions. Use these to send a thank you letter to the restaurant. Find out if any of the children have eaten in that restaurant and if so, what things they like to eat there.

Talk about the differences in eating at home and in a restaurant, and list the things the children say they like about eating out and the things they don't like about eating out.

Look over the pictures you took and make up a story about your trip to the restaurant, using your pictures and the children's comments.

Make Menus

Look at the sample menu you brought back and review the different sections of the menu, noting what kinds of foods go in each section. Cut out lots of pictures of all different kinds of foods from magazines. Use those pictures to make several menus to use in a play restaurant. Print the section headings and a few names of foods to go with the pictures. Put these together into a little booklet to resemble the type of menu you saw. If you wish, make a cover for your menu from construction paper. Print a restaurant name and the word "menu" on the cover.

~ Menu ~

Dinners
Chicken 5.95
Spaghetti & Meatballs . 6.95
Steak 10.95

Salads
Tomato & Lettuce 1.50
Chef's Special 2.50

Sandwiches
Beef Roast 3.50
Ham 2.50
Egg Salad . . 2.00
Cheese 2.50

Desserts
Pie 1.50
Cheesecake 2.00
Ice Cream . . 1.00

Beverages
Coffee .50 Tea .50 Milk .40
Pop . . .40 Lemon . . .40

Restaurant Collage

Collect a lot of ads, parts of coupons, and pictures of food items and fast food or local restaurants. Let the children make collages. They might make collages for particular types of restaurants, using the kinds of foods found in that restaurant. A collage for Burger King or McDonalds would have foods that are found there; and one for an Italian restaurant or pizza parlor would have all those types of foods.

Dramatic Play

Set up a dramatic play restaurant. Bring in a few small tables, the menus, table setting supplies (placemats and plastic silverware) centerpieces and other table items. Have the children pretend to be the chef, waitresses or waiters, hostess and customers. You can use pretend food if you have some, or make things that look like various food items out of paper, play dough, or felt and other scrap materials. If you wish, vary the type of restaurant from a family-style sit-down restaurant to a fast food restaurant or a pizza parlor. If you want to be ambitious, you can prepare some actual specialties for a day. Using items like individual pizza on English muffins, tacos, or home-baked cookies, serve lunch or snack in the pretend restaurant.

A Life Size Sorting Game

Make large master boards using 9" by 12" tagboard, and put a picture of a different kind of restaurant on each board. Include a delicatessen and different types of franchise restaurants from ice cream parlors and donut shops to steak houses. Also include some ethnic restaurants. On 3" by 5" cards, paste pictures of different foods found in those restaurants. Make one card for each food item, including everything from hamburgers, tacos, and donuts to several types of ice cream cones. A child picks a card and goes to the master board where that food would be found. The game can be played by a group, or by a few children who keep picking cards and sorting them to the appropriate master board.

Make Chef Hats

Cut a strip of white tagboard about 2" wide and almost long enough to go around the child's head. Staple a small rubber band to each end of the band. This will make the hats adjustable. Find a white paper bag with about the same circumference as the circle band. Staple the open end of the bag to the headband. Tissue paper can also be used for the hat, but is not as sturdy as a paper bag.

159

Design a Bulletin Board

Set up a restaurant bulletin board. Divide the bulletin board into two areas, the kitchen and the dining room. Put pictures of big kitchen equipment, chefs, and food being prepared in the kitchen. In the dining room area make pictures of tables and chairs, people being served and eating, stands for trays of food and so on. Draw a counter area on one side and add some display cases with pictures of fruits, cakes, pies, donuts or muffins. Pictures of food taken from boxes of packaged foods would be useful for the bulletin boards.

Planning Balanced Meals

Using pictures of food cut from magazines, plan "pretend" balanced meals. Use a paper plate and have the children tell you what to order for breakfast, lunch, and dinner. Put those pictures on your plate. Discuss those choices and whether they make a balanced meal. Let the children make balanced meal pictures on paper plates, choosing pictures of foods to eat and pasting them on their plates. Include pictures of appetizers, main courses, vegetables, fruits and dessert items. Look up the calories for some foods. On some display paper plates, write the number of calories for different foods next to the picture of the food. Write the calories for things like potato chips, donuts and pies, cookies and cakes, as well as fruits and vegetables. Explain to the children what the word "calorie" means. Talk about how many calories they need and about extra calories making fat. The next time you let the children plan the foods they choose, see if they make any changes in the things they choose.

Flannel Board Activity

Make felt cut-outs for various food items and let the children put them together. Some sample items would be white circles for buns, brown ellipses to use for hamburgers, little green circles for pickles, red and yellow drops for ketchup and mustard, and various shapes to use for hot dogs, hot dog buns, pizza and other common foods.

Songs, Poems and Fingerplays

To the tune of "I'm a Little Teapot"

The Hamburger

First you take a hamburger on a bun.
Then you start to have some fun.
Add a little ketchup and some cheese,
Lettuce and tomato, if you please.
Then you get to take a little bite.
Umm, delicious! Tastes just right!

At the Restaurant

At the restaurant, at the restaurant,
There's a menu, there's a menu.
Menu tells us what to eat,
Menu tells us what to eat.
Yum, yum, yum.

At the restaurant, at the restaurant,
There's a chef, there's a chef.
Chef who cooks the yummy food,
Chef who cooks the yummy food,
We can eat, we can eat.

At the restaurant, at the restaurant
There's a waitress, there's a waitress.
Takes our orders and brings the food,
Takes our orders and brings the food,
We can eat, we can eat.

To the tune of "Frere Jacque"

This Little Hamburger

Hold up thumb — This little hamburger has ketchup
Hold up next finger — This little hamburger has none
Hold up next finger — This little hamburger has pickles
Hold up next finger — And this little hamburger has cheese
Hold up little finger — But this little hamburger has everything
Move little finger toward mouth — And that's for me, please!

161

Five Little Children

Five little children at the restaurant today
The first one said, "I'll have steak if I may."
The second one said, "What's this I see,
Barbecue ribs, now that's for me!"

The third one said, "What should I eat?
I guess fried chicken would be a treat."

The fourth one said, "I'm not hungry,
A hamburger is enough for me."

The fifth one said, "I don't want that stuff,
But a great big pizza would be enough."

Along came the waitress,
And what do you think?
They all ordered pizza,
As quick as a wink!

Hold up five fingers to start; with the other hand touch one finger at a time — as you say each line

Can also be done with props; attach pictures of foods to tongue blades and let children hold them up in sequence

Variations on an "Old MacDonald" Theme

To the tune of "Old MacDonald had a Farm"

Old MacDonald had a hamburger,
E-I-E-I-O.
And on his hamburger he had some cheese
E-I-E-I-O.
With some cheese, cheese here,
And some cheese, cheese there,
Here some cheese, there some cheese,
Everywhere some cheese, cheese,
Old MacDonald had a hamburger,
E-I-E-I-O.

Old MacDonald had a hamburger,
E-I-E-I-O.
And on his hamburger he had some pickles
E-I-E-I-O.
With pickles here, and some cheese there,
Here a pickle, there some cheese,
Everywhere pickles and cheese,
Old MacDonald had a hamburger
E-I-E-I-O.

(Add:)
catsup, mustard, onions, and
whatever *else* the children add.

(Can also be sung:)
And *with* his hamburger
he had French fries,
a milkshake, onion rings, and so forth.

(Additional variations:)
Old MacDonald had some pizza,
E-I-E-I-O.
And on his pizza he had some cheese,
E-I-E-I-O.

(Add:)
sausage, mushrooms, green pepper,
tomato sauce, and anything else.

(And still some more variations on the same theme:)
At the restaurant they have some _____,
E-I-E-I-O.
Lettuce — (tomatoes, carrots, cucumbers and all kinds of salad ingredients)
Spaghetti — (meatballs, and everything else that goes with it)
Turkey — (stuffing, cranberry sauce, potatoes, gravy and so on)
Tacos — (lettuce, tomatoes, cheese, sour cream, beef, hot sauce, and so on)
Pancakes — (and everything that might accompany them)

And so on!

Books

Adams, Phyllis. **Pippin Eats Out.** Follett, 1982.

Black, Irma S. **Is This My Dinner?** Whitman, 1972.

Green, Carla. **I Want to be a Restaurant Owner.** Childrens Press, 1959.

Hoban, Russell and Emily Arnold McCully. **The Twenty-Elephant Restaurant.** Atheneum, 1978.

Hodgson, Louise. **Geraldine Goes to a Restaurant.** Denison.

Lerner, Mark. **Careers in a Restaurant.** Lerner, 1979.

Peters, Sharon. **Contento Juan** (Spanish). Troll, 1981.

Schwartz, Alvin. **Stores.** MacMillan, 1977.

Showers, Paul. **What Happens to Hamburger.** Crowell, 1970.

Zokeisha. **Tasty Treats.** Simon & Schuster, 1982.

Zokeisha. **Things I Like to Eat.** Simon & Schuster, 1982.

School

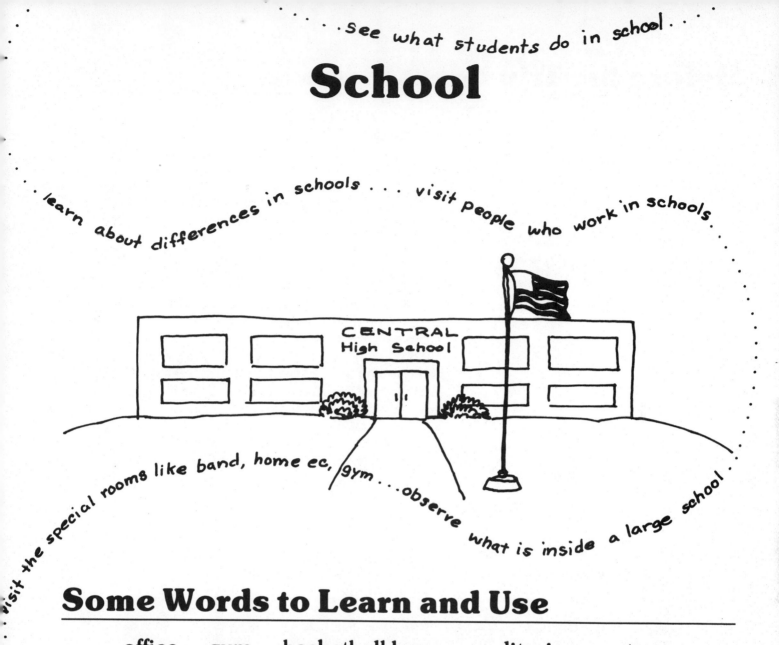

... see what students do in school ...

learn about differences in schools ... visit people who work in schools ...

visit the special rooms like band, home ec, gym ... observe what is inside a large school

CENTRAL High School

Some Words to Learn and Use

office   gym   basketball hoop   auditorium   stage

cafeteria   band room   instruments   clarinet   flute

trumpet   drum   science lab   home economics room

locker   hall   combination lock   classroom   principal

teacher   students   custodian   bell   hall monitor

trophy case   trophy   cheerleader   team   textbook

backpack   bicycle stand   parking lot   school bus   desk

counselor   media center   study carrel

Talk About

Ask the children where their older brothers and sisters go each morning. Discuss different levels of school. Ask the children what they think the big children do in school and if they would like to go to see. Ask the children if adults go to school. Ask them why people go to school.

Flannel Board Story

Make some flannel board figures of different-size children and different-sized or shaped school buildings. Match the size of the child to the size of the building as you discuss this with the children. Make up some simple stories using names of brothers and sisters in the group and names of the school buildings. For example, "Each morning Susie's sister Jane gets dressed and packs her books and goes to Sunnyside School, and Mark's sister goes to Madison Junior High." If you wish, you can add a felt school bus or some bikes to embellish your story.

On the Trip / Ideas for Exploring

Observing

Notice the general construction and the materials used in the building. Notice the grounds around the school. Is there anything outside or on the grounds to suggest that this is a school building, such as sports fields, bike racks, flag, students, playground equipment?

After entering the building, take a look around and notice the general features of the building: the long hallways lined with lockers, the central hall area with any pictures or other items on the wall, the general office area, and any trophy cases.

Walk into the office and observe the people coming and going there. Look for faculty mail boxes, telephone and intercom systems, clocks, and so on. Talk to some people who work there: student aids, the secretary, principal and counselors, to find out about the work they do.

Look carefully at the trophy case and notice the different kinds of trophies, and what they say on them. Can you tell from looking at the trophy what sport it represents?

If there are pictures of classes or teams from years ago, examine them and notice any differences in style of clothes, sports uniforms or equipment, hair or general appearances.

Notice any study carrels in the halls or other areas and talk about how they are used.

Visit the specialized areas of the school such as the gym, cafeteria, auditorium, library and media center, band room, home economics rooms, shop area and science lab. Notice the materials used in these rooms and any special construction used to make them suitable for their special purposes.

Visit the heating plant and maintenance area of the building and ask the custodians to tell you about their work.

Identifying / Demonstrating

Ask some students to show the children how the lockers look inside and how the locks work. Be sure to explain to the children the way combination locks work, if those are the types on the lockers. Have the students show the children the number and size of the books stored in the lockers. Discuss why the students need lockers.

If possible, arrange to have some students use or demonstrate for the children the things that are found in the specialized rooms of the school. Be sure to tell the children the names of the different things they see including musical instruments, gym and sports equipment, office, laboratory or audiovisual equipment. equipment.

Look for other signs of student activities or interests, such as signs on the walls, special displays, bulletin boards. Talk about the information they convey.

If there is a computer terminal in the school, ask a student to demonstrate some of the computer graphics for you and explain how the students use the computers in school.

Listening/Sensing

Notice the sounds of musical instruments played separately and together. Be sure to point out the different sounds of instruments in the same family such as the strings (from violin to double bass), woodwinds, brass and even various percussion instruments, if they have any. Wonder if the size of the instrument is related to the sound. Make some generalizations about what that relationship is. Ask the music teacher if your conclusions are correct.

Talk about the general sounds you hear in the building as you walk along. Are there bells for changing classes? Do you hear clanging lockers, singing, running, talking, clicking of typewriters, or any other sounds of students and teachers at work?

Do announcements come blaring out from time to time? Wonder where those voices come from and if you wish, go and find out how the public address system in the school works.

Notice the sounds in the gym area. Can you tell what sport is going on from the sounds you hear?

Are there any special aromas you find in some parts of the building, such as cooking smells from the home economics area, food smells from the cafeteria, coffee near the teachers' lounge, cleaning materials or fuel smells in the maintenance or shop areas?

Comparing

Make some comparisons between things you see in the school you are visiting and your group's own school or room. Talk about the older students' lockers and your children's cubbies, the home economics rooms and your housekeeping corner, the shop rooms and your workbench area. Include some of the more general items used in both situations: books, science materials, AV

materials, and so on.

   Ask the children to point out things that are familiar to them, things that are like what they use in school.

   Make some size comparisons concerning most of the equipment and features found in the school: tables, chairs, drinking fountains, shelves in the library, and point out how your own school setting is suited to young children. Wonder if all types of schools are suited to the size of their students. Discuss what happens if some students are very large or very small for their age or have some disability that makes it hard for them to use things in the building.

After the Trip / Follow-up Activities

Discussion

   Talk about the trip. Let the children share their experiences.

   Discuss with your children any similarities in things they do in school with what they see older children doing in their school. Relate these similarities and differences to the different ages and abilities of children as they grow (some samples might be power tools and big workbenches in high school shop compared to hand tools and small workbench in preschool; parallel bars and climbing ropes in school gym compared to climbing structures in preschool).

Sorting Game

   Make a sorting game using a schoolhouse shape as the masterboard and pictures cut from catalogs and mounted on cardboard as the pieces. Children match items to the appropriate room. Masterboard "rooms" should include pictures indicating the type of room.

Display

   Set up a display table of items associated with junior or senior high (trophies, combination locks, cheerleader pom-poms, some sports items, text book, gym clothes).

Cheerleading

Make megaphones out of paper or pom-poms out of crepe paper, and learn a cheer or school song that the school uses. Invite a cheerleader or some other students to visit you and have them tell what they like about their school. Have your children sing the song or cheer.

Dramatic Play

Set up a school dramatic play area: Make some lockers out of cardboard boxes. Be sure to add some pretend locks. To make locks, cut cardboard in a lock shape with a small number dial attached with a brass fastener to allow it to spin. Attach the lock handle with a paper clip so it can open.

Make paper-sack backpacks. Use some discarded school workbooks to carry in backpacks and store in lockers.

Dramatize going to different classes by ringing a bell, walking to a different area of room, pretending to work, ringing a bell, marching to another area, working.

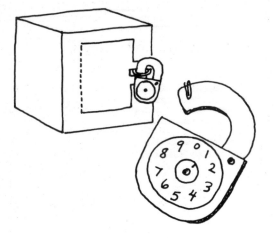

Our Book About School

Put together a booklet about your trip to school, using pictures from school supply catalogs to tell about the different rooms in the school. Include in the book photographs of students or teachers at the school, especially if they are related to any of the preschool children. Include information about the school such as colors, symbols, school teams, and subjects studied.

Mural

Make a mural of the school and surrounding area. Use cut paper shape to make the school building. Draw or use cutout figures for the students. Add school bus, flag, and playing fields to create a school scene.

Thank You Note

Write a thank-you letter to the school principal and any staff involved in rooms you visited or events you witnessed. Have the children dictate to you the things to include in the letter. Have the children make some pictures about the trip and send them along with the letter.

Songs, Poems and Fingerplays

To the tune of "Mulberry Bush"

This is the Way We Go to School

This is the way we go to school,
Go to school, go to school,
This is the way we go to school,
So early in the morning.

This is the way we open our lockers . . .
To put our things away.

This is the way we walk to class . . .
As the bell rings each day.

This is the way we go to gym . . .

This is the way we go to lunch . . .

School Bells

Ding, dong, hear the school bells ring.
See the children hurry,
Don't want to miss a thing.

Down the hall they scurry,
Loaded down with books,
Isn't it amazing,
How busy their school looks!

See the Students

See the students all in a row,	*Hold up two hands*
Marching off to class just so.	*Make hands march*
They study hard and work all day,	*Turn hands to form book*
But after school they run and play.	*Wiggle fingers and move hands to opposite sides*

Off to Class

Make motions of removing something from shoulders	Slip off the backpack, Unload all the books.
Pretend to work lock and open door	Open up the locker,
Imitate hanging up coat	Hang things on the hooks.
March around room	Now we are all ready, Off to class we go.
Sit down in front of teacher	We'll listen to our teachers,
Pretend to read a book	There's a lot to learn, you know!

171

And more

Morning Song, Mary Had a Little Lamb, from **Songs for the Nursery School.** Laura Pendleton
    MacCarteney. Willis, 1937.

Books

Adams, Phyllis. **Pippin Learns a Lot.** Follett, 1982.

Alan, Gross. **I Don't Want to Go to School.** Childrens Press, 1982.

Arnold, Caroline. **Where Do You Go to School?** Watts, 1982.

Beim, Jerrold. **Andy and the School Bus.** Morrow, 1947.

Berenstein, Stan and Jan. **The Berenstein Bears Go To School.** Random House, 1978.

Bram, Elizabeth. **I Don't Want to go to School.** Greenwillow, 1977.

Burningham, John. **The School.** Crowell, 1975.

Elliott, Dan. **Grover Goes to School.** Random House, 1982.

Feder, Paula K. **Where Does the Teacher Live?** E.P. Dutton, 1979.

Hargreaves, Roger. **Let's Play School.** Price-Stern, 1982.

Hoban, Lillian. **Will I Have a Friend?** MacMillan, 1967.

Jones, William E. and Minerva J. Goldberg. **Going to School.** Rainbow, 1978.

Kingsley, Emily. **I Like School.** Western, 1981.

Lenski, Lois. **Prairie School.** Harper & Row, 1951.

Lystad, Mary. **Jennifer Takes Over P.S. 94.** Putnam, 1972.

Oldfield, Pamela. **Melanie Brown Goes to School.** Faber & Faber, 1979.

Reif, Patricia. **The First Day of School.** Western, 1981.

Rosenblatt, Suzanne. **Everyone is Going Somewhere.** MacMillan, 1976.

Rowe, Jeanne A. **A Trip Through a School.** Watts, 1964.

Stein, Sarah B. **The School.** Doubleday, 1979.

Wells, Rosemary. **Timothy Goes to School.** Dial, 1981.

Wolf, Bernard. **Adam Smith Goes to School.** Lippincott, 1978.

Service Station

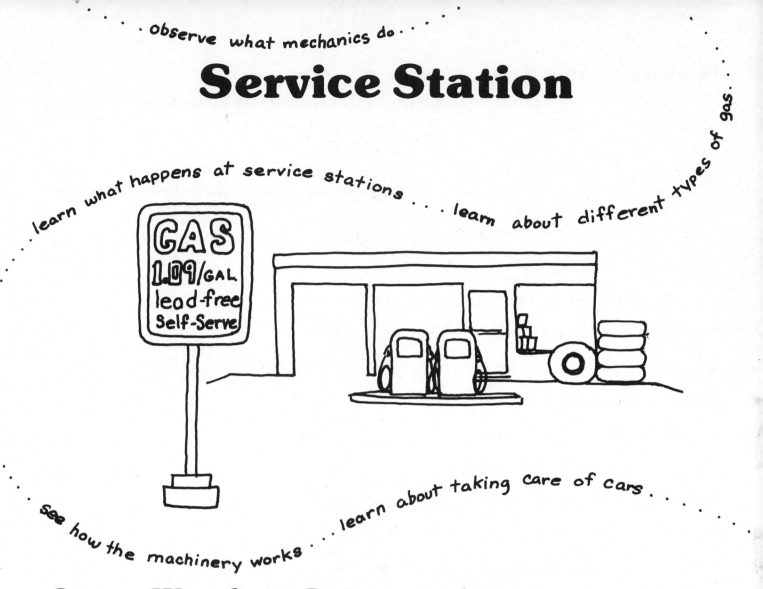

learn what happens at service stations . . . learn about different types of gas

GAS
1.09/GAL
lead-free
Self-Serve

see how the machinery works . . . learn about taking care of cars

Some Words to Learn and Use

gas pump   nozzle   hose   air pump   motor oil

gasoline   anti-freeze   mechanic   hoist   tire   air jack

battery   oil filter   lubricate   grease   tow truck

wrecker   car wash   gallon   leaded   unleaded   diesel

regular   premium   credit card   self-serve

Before the Trip / Introductory Activities

Talk About

Ask the children if they know anyone who works in a garage or service station. Have the children explain what happens at a service station. Ask the children what their parents do when something is wrong with their car. Ask the children where gasoline comes from. Have they heard their parents talk about the shortage of gasoline or its high price?

List

Make a list of questions resulting from the discussion. Include questions such as, "Where is the gas stored?", "How do the mechanics get under the car to fix it?", and others raised by the children. Plan to go to a service station to find answers.

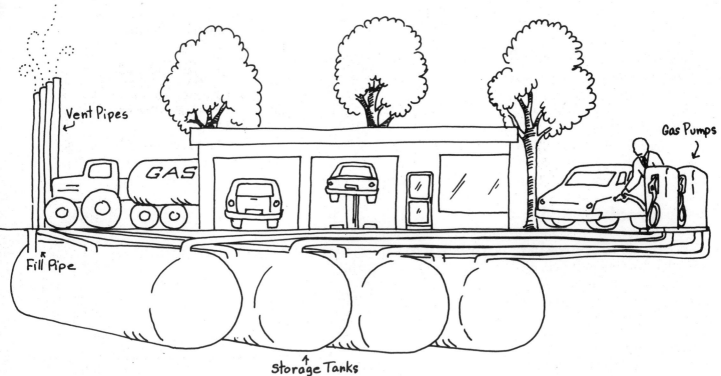

Vent Pipes

GAS

Gas Pumps

Fill Pipe

Storage Tanks

Observing

Notice the gas pump area and point out the different types of gas at the pumps. Show the children the words that tell people which pump has regular, unleaded, premium or diesel fuel. Call their attention to the beginning letters of the words and then give the pumps nicknames by type of gas, like the "R" gas, or the "UN" gas, to help them identify which one is which. When a car arrives to get some gas, see if the children can tell which kind they are getting.

Watch the numbers whirling on the pump and explain what each set of numbers tells us. Show them the dollar sign on one row so they know that one tells us how much the gas will cost. If there are self-serve and full-serve areas, look at the gas prices in each area and talk about why one costs more. Ask the children what the difference is between full and self-serve.

Look at the building on the grounds and notice how it is suited to the work that is done. Is there a garage area as well as the cashier's area? Notice the doors into each area and talk about the door for people and the doors for the cars.

Look for the name of the station and any signs or use of their logo.

If there is an automatic car wash, try to observe that in operation.

Identifying

Notice all the things around the garage and name as many as you can and ask the mechanic to tell you about some of the others. Some things to watch for and talk about are the credit-card machine, cash register, cans of oil, funnels, window cleaner, antifreeze, fan belts, tires, head lights, fuses, and other spare parts. There may even be a computer called a "diagnostic analyzer" used to tell what's wrong with a car.

Notice the tools the mechanics use and ask them to show you how some work, such as the air jack, the hoist for the cars, air gauges, air pump, tire irons, and so on. If a car is in for repair or service, try to watch it being elevated and see if you can take a peek under it.

Counting

Count the gas pumps and the number of hoses at each pump. Count the number of pumps for each type of gas.

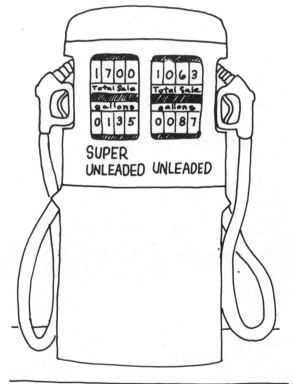

How many rows or service areas are there? How many cars can fit in each area?

Count how many people work in the service station, the number of work spaces in the garage and the number of doors.

If you wish, count how many cars you see at the station or how many tires you see in the garage.

Listening/Sensing

Listen to the clicking sounds of the gas pumps and the sounds of the gas being pumped into the car tanks.

Try the air pumps and listen to the sounds they make. If the mechanic will demonstrate the air jack, prepare the children for the very loud noise that makes. Talk about why the air makes noise when it is being pumped. Have the children practice blowing and see if they can hear that. Does it make any difference in sound when they vary how hard they blow?

What other sounds do you hear, such as traffic sounds, car horns, bells when cars drive in and out, radio, power tools? Is it a quiet or noisy place?

Notice all the smells in the garage such as fuel smells, exhaust smells, new tire smells, and special hand-cleaning soap in the bathroom. Ask the children if they like the smell of gasoline. Notice the smells in the car-wash area as well.

Speculating

Wonder where the gas comes from to get into the pumps. Ask someone to tell you where the storage tanks are. If possible, find out when the tankers deliver fresh supplies and see if you can plan to visit at that time or tell the children when it is, if it's at a time you can't visit.

Wonder why the mechanics wear special overalls and how they get their hands clean.

Talk about where all the oil, grease and general dirt in the garage comes from and wonder how they clean up the garage each day. Ask the mechanic if you can't decide.

Wonder how they fix tires. How can they find a hole in a tire to patch it? Ask a mechanic to demonstrate how they find it. Do they inflate the tire and feel where the air is coming from or do they submerge it in water and watch for bubbles? Ask the mechanic to also explain or demonstrate how they repair the tire.

Wonder if it would be fun to work in a service station. What would you have to like to do to work there?

After the Trip / Follow-up Activities

Discussion

Talk about the trip. Let the children share their experiences.

Discuss what causes tires to become flat and how they can be fixed. Let the children use a bicycle pump to inflate balloons. Stick a pin in a balloon to demonstrate how tires get punctures. How do they fix tires?

Talk about the clothes mechanics wear for their work. Why do they need heavy coveralls? Wonder how to remove grease from hands and clothes. Take some rags with grease stains on them and experiment with ways to get them clean. Does plain water remove heavy dirt? Does soaking them in soapy water work? What happens when you scrub them?

Gas Pumps, Large and Small

Make small gas pumps out of tall, thin, small cartons. Use plastic tubing or telephone cords for the hose and pump spray handles from cleaners for nozzles. Place in the block and truck area. Make a large gas pump out of larger cartons to use with trikes and wagons. Use pieces of garden hose attached at either side to make two gas lines to encourage interaction. Can be used in dramatic play area or outdoors. Set up a pretend air pump for the tires.

For the Sandbox

Build a pretend garage in sand area. Use tow trucks to tow small cars needing repairs to the garage.

A Picture Story

Have the children look for magazine pictures of things they saw at the service station. Use the cut-out pictures and descriptions dictated by the children to tell the story of what was seen on the trip or what work is done at service stations.

Matching Game

Make a matching game using service station logos cut out of magazine advertisements.

Dramatic Play

Set up an outdoor car wash for the trikes and wagons. Provide a hose with a nozzle and lots of rags for wiping and pretend waxing.

Set up a service station dramatic play interest area with cartons, gas pumps, air pumps, some tools and a few small cans such as small watering cans or oil cans (empty). Children bring cars and trucks to be checked and fixed. Children take turns being customers or mechanics at the station. Include self-service pumps, full-service pumps and a repair shop. Let the children decide on prices for the different kinds of gasoline. Mark the pumps with the different types of gas: regular, unleaded, diesel. Talk about which vehicles use which gas. Remind the children to use the diesel pump for the trucks.

Display

Set up a display of gears and talk about how they work. If you can, find some old small engines that can be taken apart to add to the display. What does oil do for old gears?

Thank-you Letter

As a group, write a thank-you letter to the station which includes statements of what the children saw on the trip. If appropriate, include some pictures the children drew after the trip.

Service Station Diorama

Make dioramas (a shoe box works well for the container) of service stations using small boxes for pumps, and the thin plastic connecting frames from toy packaging for car hoists. Attach small strips of paper folded like a spring to raise and lower the "pretend car jack." Small plastic cars can be used in the diorama.

A Visit with a Mechanic

Invite a mechanic, perhaps from the service station you visited, to visit the children and see the service station you have set up. Have the children ask the mechanic any questions they have including how they get their hands and clothes clean again, how they fix tires, and so on.

Songs, Poems and Fingerplays

To the tune of "Mulberry Bush"

Pretend to be filling gas tank

When We Go to the Station

This is the way we pump the gas,
Pump the gas, pump the gas.
This is the way we pump the gas,
When we go to the station.

Pretend to check the oil

This is the way we check the oil . . .
When we go to the station.

This is the way we wash the car . . .

This is the way we change the tires . . .

This is the way we wash the windows . . .

Pumping Gas

See the gas pumps all in a row,
Lower the hose, push the crank,
Put the nozzle in the tank,
Squeeze the handle,
And hear the gasoline flow.

Have children make motions to imitate actions described

S—s—s—s—s
Watch the pump,
Look at those numbers go!

The Gas Station

The gas station now is a whole lot more,
It's turned into a little store.
And while our car sits at the pump,
We'll run inside and then explore,
The food and games and things galore.
And while our car gets gas to eat,
We often get a different treat.

At the Station

To the tune of "Down by the Station"

Down at the service station,
Early in the morning.
See all the cars,
Awaiting in a row.
See the mechanics,
Moving them around.
Lift up the hoists,
They're off the ground!

And more

The Windshield Wiper, The Filling Station Man, from **Singing Fun.** Lucille Wood and Louise Scott. Webster, 1954.

Click Clack, from **Finger Frolics.** Liz Cromwell and Dixie Hibner. Partner, 1976.

Books

Baker, Eugene. **I Want to Be a Service Station Attendant.** Childrens Press, 1972.

Baker, Eugene. **I Want to Be an Auto Mechanic.** Childrens Press, 1976.

Benson, Christopher. **Careers in Auto Sales and Service.** Lerner, 1975.

Carlisle, Norman and Madelyn. **The True Book of Automobiles.** Childrens Press, 1965.

Clark, James. **Cars.** Raintree, 1981.

Dugan, William. **The Car Book.** Western, 1968.

Holl, Adelaide. **ABC of Cars, Trucks and Machines.** McGraw-Hill, 1970.

Lenski, Lois. **The Little Auto.** Walck, 1934.

Ottum, Bob. **Cars.** Western, 1973.

Scarry, Richard. **Cars and Trucks and Things That Go.** Western, 1951.

Shay, Arthur. **What Happens at a Gas Station.** Reily & Lee, 1972.

MORE FIELD
TRIP IDEAS

Places to Visit

Nature Resources

- camp site, woods, rock formation, small caves, mountains, waterfalls

- arboretum, botanical garden, fountain, nursery, greenhouse

- planetarium, science and natural history museum

- zoos, university animal barns, stables, fish hatchery, wildlife preserve

- hobbie farm, orchard, pumpkin patch, berry patch, poultry farm, dairy farm, egg hatchery, and other food producers

- local, county or state parks

Community Resources

- playground, recreational areas, amusement centers

- library, post office, fire station, police station, city maintenance building, community center

- telephone company, newspaper publisher, office building

- art and other special interest museums, historic houses or old buildings

- clinic (doctor, veterinarian, dentist, optometrist)

- government building, city hall, courtroom, county courthouse

- train depot, railroad yard, airport (small and large), harbor (marina or boat docking area), bus terminal

- church, synagogue, mosque

- vocational schools, special resource departments of public schools

Local Businesses or Manufacturing Areas

- food processor (peanut butter, potato chips, candy, noodles, cheese), canning plant, dairy plant, brewery or bottling plant

- grain elevator, paper mill, lumber mill

- publisher, printer

- building material suppliers (who make cement blocks, bricks, and so on)

- toy manufacturers

Stores and Service Areas

- fish market, butcher shop, ethnic grocery store, bakery, candy store (candy made on premises)

- open-air market, florist shop

- laundromat, laundry, cleaners

- beauty or barber shop, spa

- cabinet shop, electronic shop

- paint and wallpaper store, plumbing supply store

- furniture store, clock store, musical instrument store

- automobile parts store, farm implement dealership

- repair shop (TV, appliances, motors, shoes)

- pet shop

- ethnic specialty shop, sporting goods store, arts and crafts or hobby shop

- photocopier, photography shop, photographer's studio

- toy and book stores

Other

- local college (football field, stadium, gym, tennis court, pool, audiovisual department, dormitory, labs, interesting buildings, music department, furnace plant, auditorium and stage, bookstore, cafeteria)

- place with an unusual collection, artist at work, art studio

- theatre, television station, radio station

- hotel, motel, apartment building

- tall building, unusual building (concert hall, stadium, auditorium, armory, arena)

- gravel or sand pit, scrap yard, city dump, salvage yard

- bridges, dams, reservoirs and locks

- teachers' homes

- military base or service unit

- recycling center

- service site (garbage or snow removal, tree cutting, street cleaning or repairing, utility and telephone repair)

- special display in community shopping area

Trips in Reverse: Resources That Come to You

Every community boasts a large number of untapped resources, people who might be willing to share some experience with young children. To find out what is available in your community all you have to do is ask.

Family Resources

Parents, grandparents, siblings or friends may be able to demonstrate a variety of activities in the following areas:

- hobbies (anything from handicraft activities to cooking special foods or sharing collections)

- talents (musical instruments, singing, dancing, magic performances)

- ethnic costumes or cultural items, slide from travels

- pets

- occupations

- babies

- sports activities and accompanying uniforms or equipment (from fencing to football)

Community Resources

Many agencies have public relations departments which will arrange for a visit or demonstration such as:

- dairy council, county extension service agent

- firefighter with fire engine

- police officer with police car

- hospital or health personnel (nurse, lab technician, dentist, doctor)

- repair people (electrician, plumber)

- community service group (Scouts)

- arts group (theater, music)

- librarian

- reporter and photographer (newspaper, television)

- pet store personnel

- park naturalist, forest ranger

- service people (milk delivery person, mail carrier)

Techniques For Finding New Resources

—Ask the parents with whom you have contact what they would be willing to share (work, hobbies, special interests). Ask them personally or by a questionnaire. Include inquiries about grandparents or siblings who may also have things to share.

—Ask the school personnel in your area either by letter or personal contact.

—Ask the people who work in some of the community agencies mentioned above either by letter, phone call or personal contact.

—Ask the community at large through a letter or article in your local newspaper. Put a notice on the bulletin board at the grocery store or your local community center.

—Arrange for a short orientation for these visitors to let them know what to expect from preschoolers and to confer with them about their presentation to make sure it's at the right level—not too long, too complicated, or too scary for a group of young children.

Although most of these resources would be most suitable for a school or group setting, some might make for a very unusual and interesting birthday party at home.

ESPECIALLY FOR TEACHERS

Hints for Happier Trips

1. **Preparation for each trip should be made before-hand through the use of books, pictures, films or filmstrips, songs, fingerplays and group discussions.** Children should be exposed to and become familiar with the words associated with the trip and the types of things they will see. A good planning technique is to take a few minutes to write down all the words you can think of which are associated with the trip site. Choose a dozen or so that you are going to emphasize before the trip, during the trip, and afterwards. The actual announcement of a forthcoming trip shouldn't be made too far in advance because of the young child's limited understanding of time.

2. **Dramatize, through a rhythmic activity or "homemade" story, the actual process of going on a trip.** Detail such things as getting on a bus or in a car, sitting on the bus, looking out the window, getting off the bus, holding partners' hands and walking in a group to the destination, meeting the people at the trip site, hearing noises children might notice, going back to the bus, returning to the school or house. This trial run helps the children understand what will happen and makes the actual process more meaningful. It also reduces the anxiety involved in leaving a familiar setting and going to an unknown one.

3. **When going to a special place, plan the trip carefully with the person in charge of the place you will be visiting.** It is best to visit the site ahead of the trip and learn the type of information the children will be getting and what they will see. Find out what you can do and what the resource person at the site will do. If appropriate, alert that person to the nature of young children. Make sure the information is age-appropriate and that children will be able to see things in small groups. Discourage people from giving long lectures to young children. Notice the physical setup (where the bus should stop or you should park, what door to come in, bathroom locations, and good places for regrouping or snacking). The more familiar you are with the site, the more you can help make the introduction and on-site comments suitable for your group. If possible, take a few pictures of the site to show to the children as you discuss your impending visit.

4. **If necessary, arrange for extra help on the trip.** When establishing the adult-child ratio, consider the ages of the children and their personalities. Keep in mind that children can get much more out of a trip if they can talk about it with an adult and get answers to their questions. This requires added attention and help. Make sure you have given each helper some orientation. Let them know the specific purpose and objectives of this trip and what they will be seeing en route. This will help them talk about the trip with the children.

5. **Let parents know about the trip both before and after.** Permission slips or a note about the proposed trip, date, and time are necessary. After the trip a newsy note home on what the children have seen helps parents reinforce the experience. Encourage parents to come along on trips as this helps the parents learn what to point out to children. It also helps the child feel more secure, and allows the parent a meaningful way of helping and participating in the child's day care experience.

6. **Remember that children who are anxious in new situations and accept change reluctantly are apt to find a trip frightening or may not want to go.** Such children need extra support, comfort and individual attention on trips. These children should be with the teacher, caregiver or a familiar adult. It is wise to consider inviting the parents of these children along, to help insure a smooth experience, especially in the beginning. Volunteers should be alerted to watch for signs that a child is becoming anxious and to physically comfort that child. It is not a good idea to undertake trips of any distance the first few weeks the children are with you. Give them time to become thoroughly familiar with their new setting and with you before venturing too far away.

7. **Trips provide a wealth of new experiences, but new experiences can sometimes be frightening even to the most well-traveled child.** Whenever possible, anticipate sounds and/or situations which might frighten the children. Prepare them by talking about the potentially frightening thing, and/or dramatizing it, in advance. For example, "Some animals make loud noises. Let's all oink as loud as we can to see what it might sound like at the farm." These things can be done in the home or classroom and again en route to the site. Discuss what to do if the sound occurs (cover ears, laugh, jump three times, or all of these). All of these activities will help prevent tears and fright, which could mar the entire trip. Although it is not possible to guess ahead of time what may prove frightening to a particular child, it is worthwhile to identify some potentially frightening aspects and think of ways to prepare the children for them.

8. **Following a trip be sure to allow plenty of time for discussion as well as a dramatic play situation related to the trip.** Children assimilate new knowledge by using it in play. Thus follow-up activities become an important part of the learning that can occur through field trips. Try to bring something back from each trip that can be used in follow-up activities. Keep some appropriate souvenirs or pictures of the trip to refresh the children's memories about it later on. Bring along a camera and take pictures of the children during the trip to display later on a bulletin board or for use in a homemade story about your trip.

A carefully planned and executed field trip program can enrich the children's learning and broaden their horizons. Without careful planning and follow-up, however, many of these learning opportunities are lost.

What Would You Do If?
—Some Possible Solutions

You are taking your group of children on their monthly field trip and have made necessary arrangements, but what would you do if. . .?

1. You are visiting the local television station and an emergency news announcement has delayed the program you are scheduled to visit.

   a. **Take an informal tour around the waiting area or the outside of the building.**

b.   Sing some songs, do some fingerplays or read a story from your emergency "bag of tricks."

c.   Pretend you are putting on a television show and have the group participate.

2.   You are en route home and your vehicle has a flat tire.

a.   If the location is safe, let the children watch the changing of the tire.

b.   If the group must wait for help, locate a safe area nearby or keep the children in the vehicle. Sing songs, do some fingerplays, or read stories. Have a snack from your emergency "bag of tricks."

3.   As you approach the chicken coop at the farm, one of the children becomes very frightened and won't go any closer.

a.   Stay with the child yourself or assign someone else to remain with the child. Don't force the child to go closer. Practice making chicken sounds and wonder if there are eggs to see. Offer encouragement. If the child is willing, suggest going closer, taking a peek and leaving quickly.

b.   Allow the child to remain at a comfortable distance. Avoid all shame and coaxing, but let the child know it is okay to come closer when he or she feels ready.

4.   You have just left for a neighborhood walk after carefully instructing the children to stay together. Two children run ahead of the group.

a.   This would be a good time to firmly establish the rule of not running ahead. Immediately end the walk. *Control on trips is essential and establishing good control requires strong reinforcement.* When back in school or home, practice walking together as a group. When the group learns to walk together, take another walk. If the children stay together, be sure to acknowledge their learning to stay together. When you return from the walk, again express your appreciation of their responsible behavior by telling them that you liked the way they took care of themselves by staying together, and that now the group can go on more outings.

b.   Write a story about both experiences, i.e. the time they had to come back and this time. Write up and illustrate a simple list of procedures for going on walks: we stay together, we hold hands, and we stop at the corner.

Safety-Proofing Your Trips

1. Be sure all children are wearing name tags which include the name and phone number of the school or day care provider. For large groups, color code the name tags so children and their specific group leaders have tags of the same color.

2. Trips should be undertaken only after good group control has been established and children have learned to remain with the group. Before taking your first neighborhood excursion, plan one or two trial runs. Return immediately if any children run ahead of the group.

3. Plan trips for the middle of the week to allow planning with children and return of permission slips. Avoid taking trips on Mondays, when children are apt to be tired from the weekend and not completely re-oriented to the group, or on Fridays, when follow-up activities are not possible. Plan excursions for the morning when children are less tired.

4. Establish simple safety rules which are well-known to the children and the adults accompanying them. Help children learn these rules by rehearsing or playing them out during several days before a trip. Review them immediately before departing. Some sample safety rules:

   —Always wait for the adults before crossing streets or going into buildings.

   —Everyone holds hands.

   —Always walk and never run on trips.

   —Everyone needs to sit down on the bus or in the car.

   —For groups of 10 or more: "A leader in the front and a leader in the back and all the children in between." This makes a nice chant to use as you walk along.

5. Orient other adults to safety procedures and remind them to:

   —Be conscious of the number of children they are responsible for and count noses frequently.

   —Concentrate on the children in their care and avoid being distracted by conversations with other adults.

   —Never leave children alone or send them ahead of the group for any purpose. If necessary, the whole group goes into the bathroom together.

   —Take the children to the bathroom before leaving on a trip and, if necessary, before leaving the trip site to return.

   —Supervise toileting in public places very carefully.

6. A first-aid kit should be taken along on a trip. Tape an index card of emergency numbers to the top (paramedics and poison control center). Be sure the kit includes materials for cleansing scrapes and bruises, and plenty of bandaids. Take along the parent permission slips for this trip. They include the phone numbers where parents could be reached in an emergency, or make a list of phone numbers for inclusion in the kit.

7. Take along an emergency "Bag of Tricks" for any special situation. Items to include in this bag are: a few sets of extra clothes, tissues, a few story books, and a box of graham crackers or raisins for an extra snack in case of unexpected delay. Include some instant playthings packed in individual plastic bags such as: crayons, small spiral notebooks, small pleated muffin paper cups, one foot pieces of yarn, pipe cleaners, styrofoam packing pellets and toothpicks.

8. If a snack is to be served on the trip, plan it carefully for ease of serving. Fresh fruits like apples or bananas are easier to serve than juice and crackers. Carry snacks in disposable bags so your load will be lighter on the return trip. The bags can also be used for treasures collected on the trip. If the trip is during lunch time, pack lunches in individual disposable paper bags. If lunches are sent from home, names should be on the bags. Discourage carrying anything that must be cared for and returned, such as lunch boxes or thermos bottles. Beverages should be provided for the group. Be sure to bring paper cups, napkins and a can opener if you are serving juice. A damp cloth in a plastic bag or some moist towelettes can come in very handy.

9. Plan the adult-child ratio carefully. Suggested ratios are:
   For two-year-olds: one adult to two children
   For three-year-olds: one adult to four children
   For four- and five-year-olds: one adult to five children.

   If a large group is going, plan to have one adult who is not responsible for any children. That person can be responsible for supervising the logistical arrangements at the site and such things as snacks and personal belongings brought along on the trip. This person would also be available to cope with any sudden emergencies without endangering supervision of the total group.

10. Check insurance policies to make sure they include coverage during excursions away from your home or school and en route. Also check your coverage for volunteers accompanying the group and for anyone providing transportation.

11. If a large group is going by bus, send one car to the trip site to be used in the event of any emergency or mechanical trouble with the bus.

12. When walking with very young children or in hazardous situations, it may be advisable to use a knotted or looped walking rope as an added precautionary measure. Each child holds on to a knot or loop on the rope.

Sample Forms

GENERAL PERMISSION SLIP

Dear Parent:

    An important part of our regular program includes walks in the neighborhood and a few field trips into the community. These are an excellent means of expanding children's knowledge of the world around them. Children are always well supervised on excursions. Please sign and return the enclosed permission slip for our records.

                                        Sincerely,

_____

- -

_____ has my permission to go on neighborhood

walks and community field trips while attending _____ program.

_____   _____

Date   Parent Signature

SPECIFIC NOTIFICATION AND PERMISSION SLIP

Dear Parents,

We are planning a trip to the Community Nature Center on Thursday, May 15. We will be leaving at 9:30 a.m. and returning at 11:30 a.m. Several parents have volunteered to accompany us, so we will have enough supervision for the children to explore the center in small groups. Please dress your child in old clothes suitable for exploring woods and dirt. Be sure your child is wearing a long sleeve shirt, long pants and an old sweater or jacket. Please do not send any money with your child. We will provide a snack while at the center and will not allow any of the children to buy candy or pop from the vending machines in the building. If no one has any money we will not have to impose any restrictions. We thank you for your cooperation.

We hope to see many of the early blooming shrubs and sapping of the maple trees. There are also many small animals and birds on view at the center. If we are lucky, we will see beavers at work in the pond area as well as many frogs and toads. We hope this information will help you interpret any comments your child may bring home, since children often give graphic, but confusing reports such as having seen "trees milked" or "some jumping things."

Sincerely yours,

_____

Please sign and return the field trip permission slip below.

- -

Date _____

_____ *has my permission to participate in the field*

trip to ___(Community Nature Center)___ *on* ___(May 15th)___.
                  Place   *Date*

_____   _____
Parent Signature   *Phone number of parent during the trip.*

FIELD TRIP PLANNING FORM

Type of Walk _____

Purpose _____

Words Associated With Walk _____

_____

Introductory Activity or Question _____

_____

Things to Watch for or Collect on Walk _____

_____

_____

Follow-up Activities _____

_____

_____

Songs _____

_____

Books _____

_____

Poems or Fingerplays _____

_____

Anticipated Problems _____

_____

Is a Revisit Appropriate? _____

  Purpose _____

  Activity _____

FIELD TRIP CHECKLIST FOR DAY CARE PROVIDER

	Field Trip Site	Phone No.	Date	Time Schedule
A	_____	_____	_____	_____
B	_____	_____	_____	_____
C	_____	_____	_____	_____
D	_____	_____	_____	_____
E	_____	_____	_____	_____

Transportation Arranged / Extra Help Secured (Name and Phone No.)

Trip A _____

Trip B _____

Trip C _____

Trip D _____

Trip E _____

Special Needs

Trip A _____

Trip B _____

Trip C _____

Trip D _____

Trip E _____

	Trip A	Trip B	Trip C	Trip D	Trip E
Parent Notices Complete	_____	_____	_____	_____	_____
Site Arrangements Complete	_____	_____	_____	_____	_____
Name Tags Organized	_____	_____	_____	_____	_____
Planning Forms Complete for All Adults on Trip	_____	_____	_____	_____	_____
First-Aid Kit Ready	_____	_____	_____	_____	_____
Bag of Tricks Ready	_____	_____	_____	_____	_____
Snack for Trip	_____	_____	_____	_____	_____
Permission Slips Returned	_____	_____	_____	_____	_____

ORIENTATION LIST FOR VOLUNTEERS

1. Thank you for helping make this exciting experience possible.

2. Familiarize yourself with the information sheet for this specific trip. It will tell you the purpose of the trip, points of interest to talk about en route, and special words to explain to the children.

3. You will supervise five children. Their name tags and yours are the same color. You might play a little game with the children to help you learn their names. Try to relate personally to each child, making sure each one feels comfortable.

4. Some children may feel unsure in new situations. Comfort them, hold their hands, smile. Talk about how fun it is to go away for a little while and then *return* and tell others about it.

5. During the course of the field trip, talk with your group of children about what they are seeing. Frequently repeat the names of things, and also repeat or retell information that may be given by a guide. Encourage questions and stimulate curiosity with your own questions. "I wonder how that works?" "Why do you think she is doing that?"

6. Anticipate situations such as puddles, mud or obstacles in the path. Prepare children so impending difficulties may be avoided. Tell the children what to do, such as "Take a big, big step over the puddle" instead of saying "Don't step in the puddle."

7. Each class and group should stay together. Watch for children who may need individual attention and supervise them closely.

8. Children must be with adults at all times! They should not be left alone or sent alone to find another group or teacher. This can become a frightening experience, and should be avoided. Go to the bathroom as a group, if necessary, or find another adult to supervise the children who are waiting.

9. Stay calm and relaxed. Your calmness will reassure children in any situation. Remember, most problems can be solved with a few moments of calm thinking. Play little games such as "I Spy Something Red" or "What Do I See?" in situations where children have to wait and are growing restless.

10. Have fun. Enjoy what you're doing and share your enthusiasm. Then the children will share your enjoyment.

Please note: If you prefer, this could be written in a letter format.

SUGGESTED RESOURCES

Field Trips

Buschhoff, Lotte. *Going on a Trip.* Baker, Katherine Reed (Ed.) **Ideas That Work With Young Children.** NAEYC, 1972. The article discusses general considerations in planning field trips. Children's feelings, the adult's role and what children can learn are discussed. Interesting trips are suggested, particularly ordinary work experiences.

Carson, Rachel. **Sense of Wonder.** Harper & Row, 1956. The author stresses that those who live with the mysteries of earth, sea and sky are never alone or weary of life. Her narrative and photographs explore how a child, with the companionship of an adult, can discover the joy and excitement of our world.

Cherry, Clare et. al. **Nursery School Management Guide.** Fearon, 1973. A useful guide for all areas of nursery school or day care management. A section on field trips includes sample forms, notification letters, and checklists.

Landreth, Catherine. **Preschool Learning and Teaching.** Harper & Row, 1972. A section on field trips is included in this introduction to early childhood education. Suggestions of many places to visit are related to children learning about their community. How children learn and ways of fostering learning are thoroughly discussed.

Maryland State Department of Health and Mental Hygiene. *Trips* in **Child Day Care Guidelines,** 1976. (Department of Health and Mental Hygiene, Preventive Medicine Administration, P.O. Box 13528, Baltimore, MD 21203.) An easy-to-read, well organized resource on many aspects of child care. The section on trips discusses the purpose of trips, places to visit and length of trips. Suitable trips for children under three years of age to six-years-old are suggested. Helpful suggestions for adults are included.

Mitchell, Grace. **I Am! I Can!** Grelock, 1977. The author discusses the broad spectrum of operating a child care center, and includes many curriculum ideas. The section concerning field trips contains many helpful suggestions and ideas for trips.

Taylor, Barbara J. **A Child Goes Forth.** Brigham Young University, 1972. The text presents many curriculum planning methods and ideas. The chapter on field trips contains many ideas for trips and planning suggestions. The author also recommends many children's books on a variety of topics.

General Reference List

Childcraft—The How and Why Library. Field Enterprises Educational Corporation.

The World Book Encyclopedia. Field Enterprises Educational Corporation.

The Book of Knowledge. Grolier International, Inc.

These encyclopedias all have excellent pictures and informative articles on many of the trip topics.

Curriculum Planning and Children's Learning

Broad, Laura Peabody and Nancy Towner Butterworth. **The Playgroup Handbook.** St. Martin's, 1974. The text is designed for parents involved in play groups. Activities are suggested for every month of the year. Each month includes suggestions for a possible trip.

Flemming, Bonnie Mack, et. al. **Resources for Creative Teaching in Early Childhood Education.** Harcourt Brace, 1977. This extensive curriculum guide is organized into topics. Each topic contains a wealth of activity suggestions and background information. Some topics include field trip ideas.

Singer, Dorothy and Tracey A. Revenson. **A Piaget Primer.** International Universities, 1978. Many of Piaget's theories about children's thinking are presented in an easy-to-read format. Examples supporting the theories are often quotes from classic children's books and popular comic strips.

Fingerplays, Songs and Children's Books

Cromwell, Liz and Dixie Hibner. **Finger Frolics.** Partner, 1976. A compilation of old and new favorite fingerplays on a wide variety of topics.

Grayson, Marion F. **Let's Do Fingerplays.** David McKay, 1962. An extensive selection of fingerplays organized by topics.

MacCarteney, Laura Pendelton. **Songs for the Nursery School.** Willis, 1937. Short songs for two-year-olds to more complex songs for five-year-olds are contained in this old, but valuable book. Many of the songs are action songs.

Scott, Louise Binder and J. J. Thompson. **Rhymes for Fingers and Flannelboards.** McGraw-Hill, 1960. Two hundred thirty-two fingerplays grouped by subject areas. Some may require adapting for non-sexist and multicultural awareness. Some fingerplays are written in other languages as well as English.

Subject Guide to Children's Books in Print. R. R. Bowker, Annual. This volume contains an extensive list of children's books, grouped by topic. Not annotated.

Wood, Lucille and Roberta McLaughlin. **Sing a Song: Of Holiday and Seasons, Home, Neighborhood and Community.** Prentice-Hall, 1960. Many catchy tunes about the community and seasons are included in this book. They are easy to sing and play.

Wood, Lucille and Louise Scott. **Singing Fun and More Singing Fun.** Webster, 1954. These older but useful books contain many songs about the community. Many have been recorded by Bowmar Records.